# Saint Augustine Lights

## Reflections on the Ancient City

Pastels by

Thomas E Higgins

and

Judith Alapi Higgins

Ponce de Leon's
1513 Travels

# Ponce De Leon's First Voyage

The Silk Road was a network of trade routes that provided Europeans access to the riches of the "East Indies" (the name Europeans used for Asia). In 1453, the Ottoman Turks took Constantinople and the Silk Road became difficult and dangerous. The Portuguese then developed a sea route around the African Cape of Good Hope to the Indies.

On August 3, 1492, Christopher Columbus set sail from Spain on a quest to find a western sea route to the Indies. He had the appointment by King Ferdinand and Queen Isabella as Admiral of the Ocean Seas and Governor of new lands he could claim for Spain. He stopped first at the Canary Islands to restock his provisions before setting sail west on September 6. At about 2 AM on October 12, lookouts on the Pinta spotted land in what is now the Bahamas.

Columbus found that the natives, who they called Indios, wore gold ear decorations, which spurred the explorers to search for their source. Columbus explored the northern coasts of Cuba and Hispanola (present day Haiti and Dominican Republic), on which he grounded and lost the Santa Maria. After leaving 39 men as settlers in Fort La Navidad, Hispanola, Columbus left the "West Indies" and returned to Spain on the Nina, arriving on March 15, 1493.

On September 24, 1493, Columbus set out from Spain with a fleet of 17 ships carrying 1,200 men and women to establish colonies in the newly discovered lands. Juan Ponce de Leon (Juan, the Lion Prince) accompanied Columbus on this second voyage. Columbus found that in his absence, Fort La Navidad had been ransacked, and the inhabitants dead or missing. He then sailed eastward and set up the colony, La Isabella.

Ponce de Leon led a successful campaign to crush an Indio's rebellion on the east side of the island, and was rewarded with a provincial governorship and prospered. He learned from the Indios that the nearby island of San Juan Bautista (present Puerto Rico) was a fertile land with much gold in its many rivers. With thoughts of its riches, Ponce de Leon requested and received permission for an expedition to the island. Returning to Hispanola with much gold, Ponce de Leon was appointed Governor of San Juan.

Ponce de Leon and his fellow settlers put the Indios to work growing food and mining for gold. Ponce de Leon prospered in his governorship, but politics changed when a new Viceroy for the West Indies appointed new officers for the colony which made Ponce de Leon's position on the island untenable and he was replaced.

In compensation for losing his governorship, Ponce de Leon was given a contract to explore and settle the undiscovered islands to the north. He equipped three ships and set out from San Juan with over 200 men on March 4, 1513 and sailed northwest along the Bahamas.

On April 2, 1513, he discovered what he thought was a large island that he named La Florida in honor of the Pascua Florida, or Feast of Flowers (Easter). The following day he came ashore in what is now Saint Augustine, according to some historians.

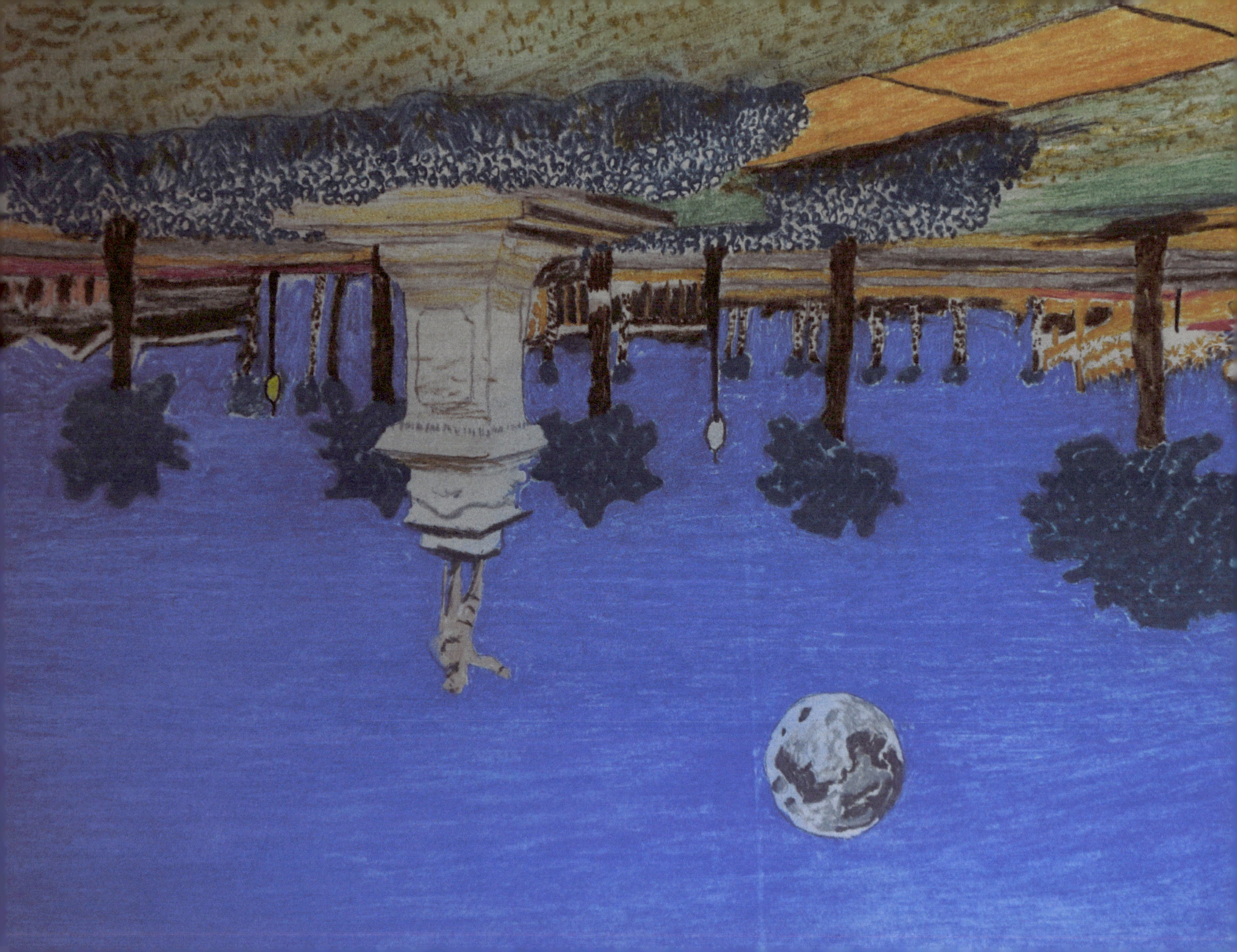

# Ponce De Leon's Statue in Front of The Bridge of Lions

After remaining around the initial landing site for 5 days, Ponce de Leon and his crew turned south exploring their new-found island. They reached and named Biscayne Bay, and landed on an island to take on water and explored the Miami River, before sailing west along the Florida Keys. Finding a gap in the reefs, they sailed Northwest, along the western coast of La Florida, landing south of Tampa Bay. Heading south again, they encountered hostile natives in war canoes near Sanibel Island. They continued their exploration before returning to Puerto Rico, after being gone for eight months.

Ponce de Leon travelled to Spain, where a new contract was awarded to him confirming his rights to settle and govern Bimini and Florida. In 1521, Ponce de Leon organized a colonizing expedition of 200 men on two ships. The expedition landed on the coast of southwest Florida, but was attacked by native warriors. Ponce de Leon was wounded by a poison arrow, and died of his wounds. The colony attempt was abandoned, and Ponce de Leon's body returned to Puerto Rico for burial.

Following Ponce de Leon's death, Spain's kings authorized a dozen expeditions to colonize La Florida. Spanish colonies survived briefly at San Miguel de Guadalupe and Pensacola, but all failed.

The Spanish colonies in Mexico and South America returned fortunes in gold to Spain. France and Spain fought a 65 year war over control of Italy during this period, and French pirates and colonists threatened the Spanish colonies and treasure ships returning to Spain. Spain and France had signed the Treaty of Cateau-Cambresis in 1559, giving Spain control of Italy and affirmed Spain's sole right to colonize La Florida.

Spain was interested in La Florida mainly because treasure ships returned to Spain with help from the Gulf Stream between Florida and the Bahamas. They feared that French settlements could harbor pirates who would attack these treasure ships.

In 1563, King Philip of Spain received word from spies in France that France was attempting to establish a colony in La Florida. The King ordered the Captain of his Indies fleet, Pedro Menendez de Aviles, and Cuba's governor to investigate, and that any French settlement be destroyed. The governor sent a ship to search for French settlements. They found evidence of an abandoned colony in what is now South Carolina.

King Philip decided that it was necessary to renew Spain's efforts to colonize La Florida, despite the previous 12 failed attempts. The King enlisted Pedro Menendez de Aviles in the effort, and hoped that Menendez would finance the effort himself.

The agreement reflected Menendez's concerns of the risks of another colonization effort. He received huge land grants, annual salary, and other concessions that would pass to his descendants. In exchange, Menendez was required to establish two or three Spanish towns in Florida.

In addition to the financial rewards, Menendez hoped to find his son, Juan, who had been lost in a shipwreck off the coast of La Florida. On March 26, a few days after the contract with Menendez was signed, word was received that a new French colony was being established in Florida.

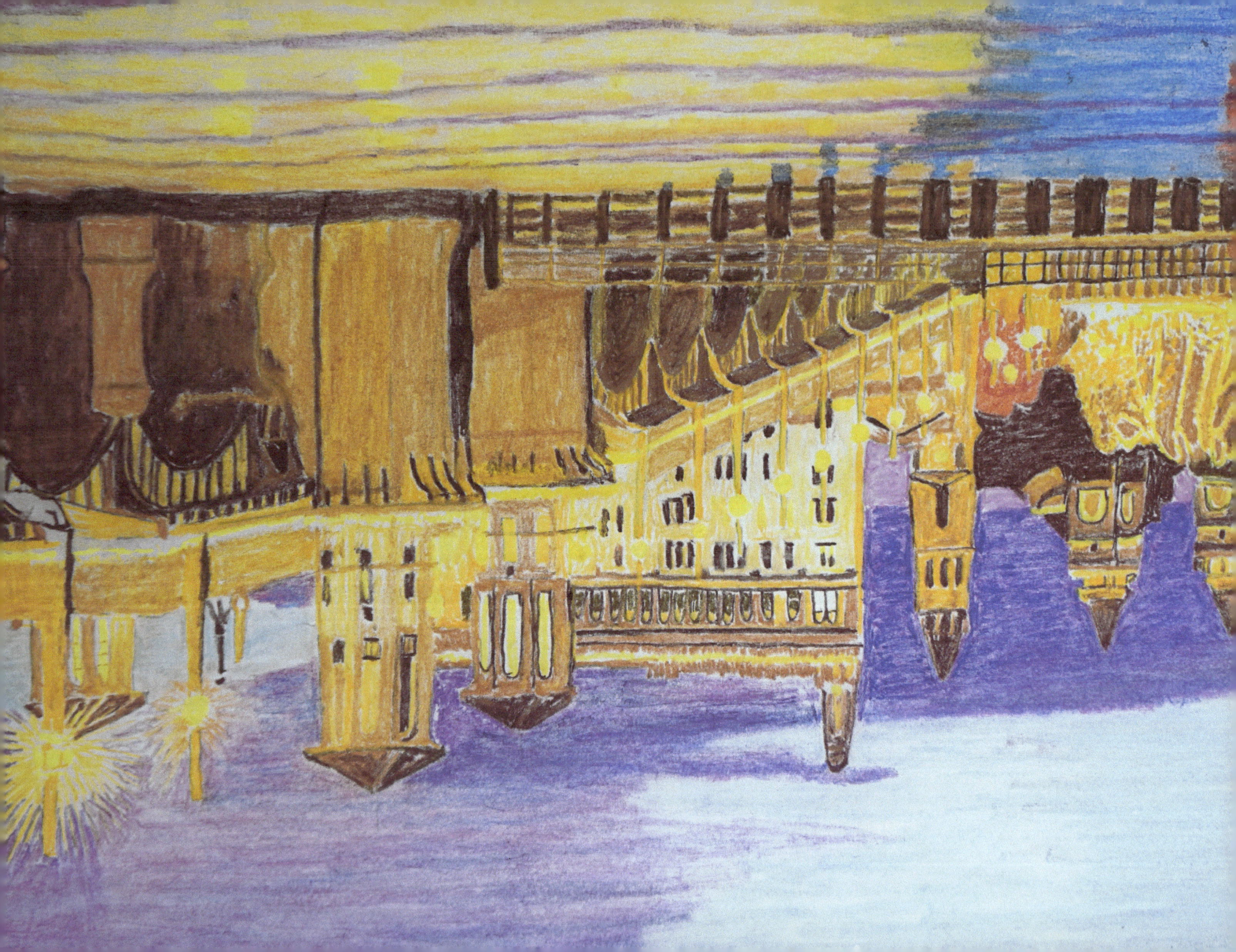

# The Bridge of Lions

The Bridge of Lions connects St Augustine and Anastasia Island across Matanzas Bay. It is named for Ponce de Leon, who first sighted the area in his exploration of La Florida. Two Carrara marble lions, Firm and Faithful, guard the entrance to the bridge from the city. Two additional granite lions, modelled after Firm and Faithful, were added to the eastern end of the bridge on July 2, 2015.

The bridge is constructed as a series of arches, with a center double draw bridge that opens to accommodate sailboats and other tall ships.

Construction of the bridge began in 1925 and was completed in 1927. It replaced an earlier wooden bridge. It was constructed as a work of art, not merely to carry cars, costing an order of magnitude more than nearby purely functional bridges.

The bridge aged and frequently broke down. In 2004, a temporary bridge was constructed next to the original structure, and used while the Bridge of Lions was restored, returning to service on March 17, 2010. The bridge has been called "The Most Beautiful Bridge in Dixie." Roads and Bridges magazine named it fourth in the nation's top bridges in 2010.

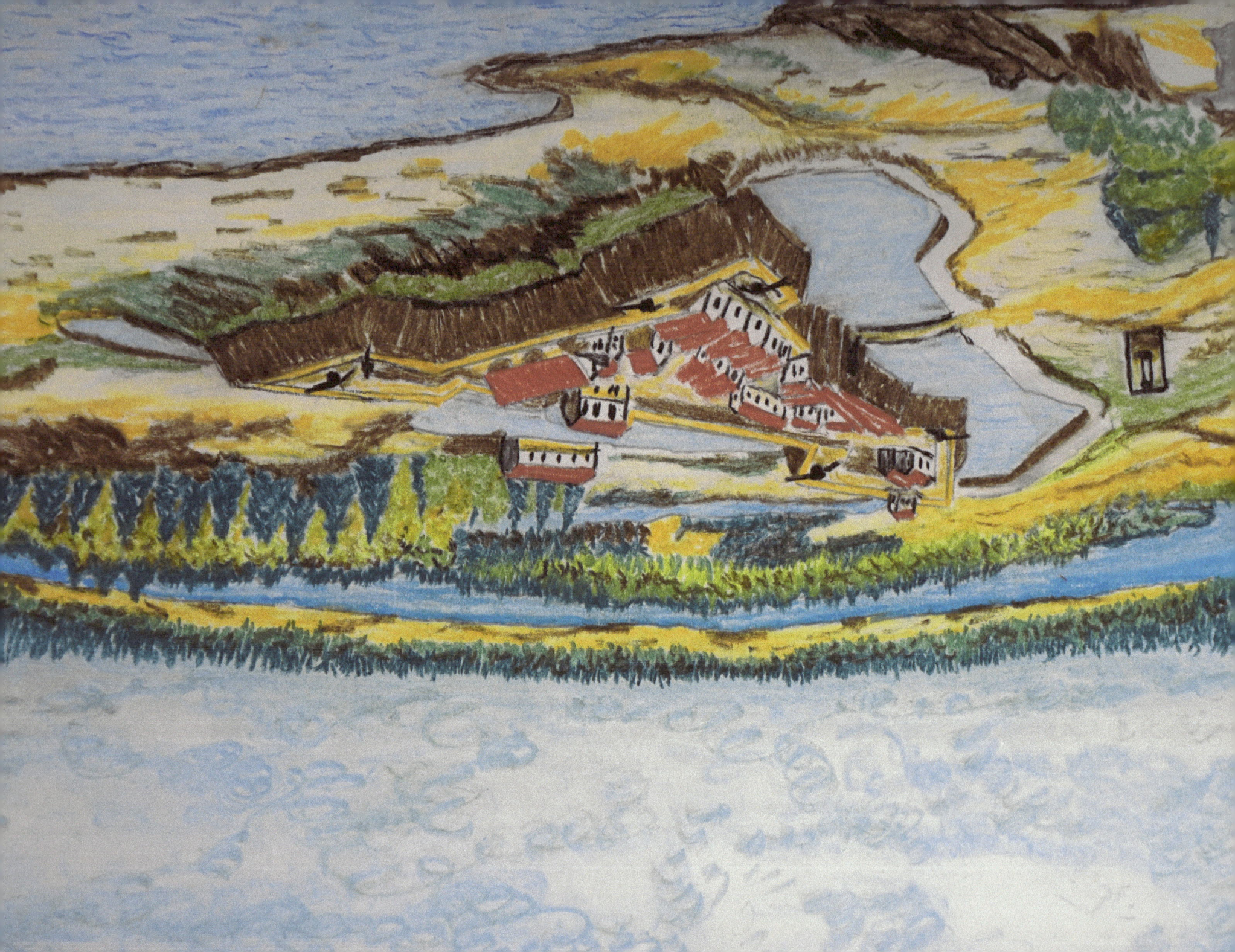

# Fort Caroline

On April 22, 1564, Rene de Laudonniere had sailed to what is now Jacksonville and established a settlement he called Fort Caroline, on the St John's River. In addition, news from France was that French reinforcements were being sent to Fort Caroline under the command of Captain Jean Ribault.

King Philip changed Menendez's contract and provided more ships and soldiers and expedited the expedition, which was to attack Fort Caroline and expel the French from La Florida.

On June 29, 1565, Menendez departed Spain with a fleet of nineteen ships and more than 1,000 soldiers and settlers. While crossing the Atlantic, he encountered a fierce storm for 3 days, which forced him to jettison most of his cannons. He arrived at Puerto Rico, with just four of his ships. He added a ship and additional soldiers to his expedition and set off for La Florida.

His fleet sighted Florida around Cape Canaveral, and sailed North, they spotted a good harbor, which Menendez called St Augustine. The fleet continued North cautiously in search of the French Colony. They found Fort Caroline, guarded by four French ships.

Menendez realized that his heavily laden ships, in poor shape from the storms were vulnerable. He therefore retreated to the good harbor that he had spotted earlier. After unloading men and supplies, he presided over a ceremony establishing the colonial town of St Augustine.

At Fort Caroline, Jean Ribault collected a force of 600 soldiers, and 5 of his largest ships plus smaller vessels and set out to attack the Spanish forces. Seeing the French ships off the coast, Menendez sent his two largest ships back to Hispanola, rather than risk their capture. As Menendez built defenses, a northeasterly wind began to blow, and the French vessels headed out to sea, to avoid grounding. They then chased the two Spanish vessels heading to Hispanola.

Fortunately for Menendez, the French vessels were forced southward by the storm, leaving Fort Caroline unprotected. The Northeastern winds also prevented Menendez from sailing north to take the fort.

Using local Indians and a captured Frenchman as guides, Menendez took a force of 500 soldiers and headed overland in the raging storm north to Fort Caroline, through flooded swamps and dense brush.

The French settlers at Fort Caroline felt that they were protected by the storm, and slept peacefully. Guards were relieved of their duties due to the severity of the storm.

Menendez and his soldiers attacked the undefended fort at dawn, their sounds deadened by the falling rain, catching most of the garrison in their beds. When they woke up , they attempted to surrender, but were slaughtered. Women and children were spared, but 142 men died by swords.

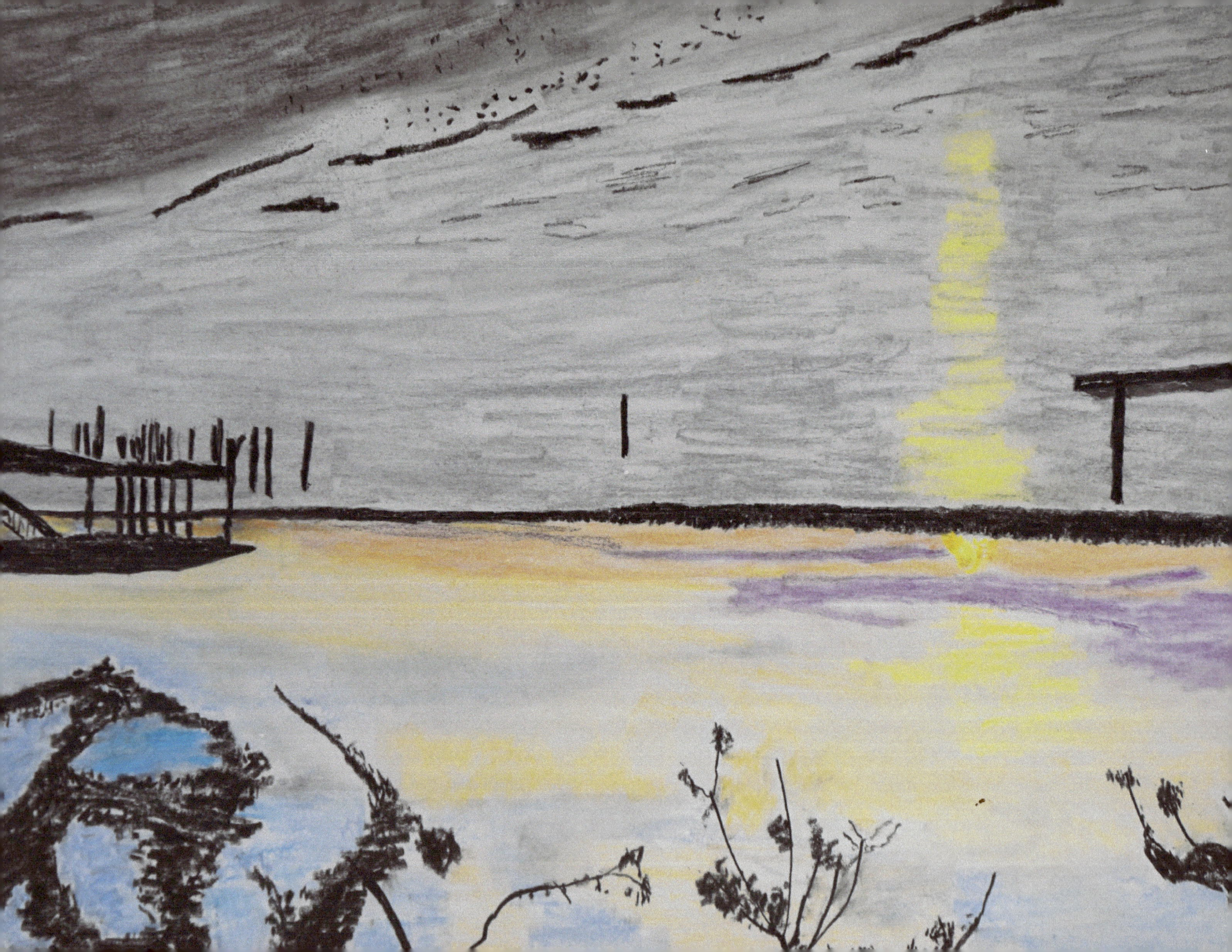

# The Matanzas River at Sunset

Fifty women and children and some 30 to 60 men were put on two of the captured French vessels and returned to France. Following the victory, Menendez destroyed the fort and left 300 soldiers to guard a new fort, San Mateo, and returned with the rest of his soldiers to St Augustine.

St Augustine celebrated the defeat of the French at Fort Caroline, but worried about the French fleet. Four of the five ships were stranded or wrecked and the surviving crew attempted to return overland to Fort Caroline, not realizing that it had been captured by Menendez.

The Spanish learned from local Indians that the French were stranded on a barrier island, eighteen miles south of St Augustine. Menendez assembled a force of some fifty men and headed south to meet the French. The two forces faced each other across what is now the Matanzas Inlet.

The French confided that the French fleet was lost, and that they were shipwrecked and exhausted, suffering from days without eating. In the following negotiations, Menendez informed the ranking French officer that Fort Caroline had been captured, and that the men had been killed. The French Captain begged for his and his men's lives.

Menendez asked if the French were Catholic or Huguenots, which the French responded that they were Huguenots. Menendez promised that he would let God decide the Frenchmen's fate if they surrendered their weapons and put themselves at His mercy. The French surrendered themselves to the Spaniards. Menendez arranged to ferry 10 French at a time, across the inlet. There they were fed and sent north to a distance out of sight or hearing to the other French, where they were put to the sword.

Two weeks later, word reached St. Augustine that the force of French under the command of Captain Jean Ribault, was stranded at the Matanzas Inlet. Menendez took a force of 150 men and headed south to meet them. After the French were informed of the loss of Fort Caroline, they agreed to surrender. After they were disarmed and fed, their hands were tied behind them, marched to the location of the previous massacre, and put to the sword.

The Matanzas River and inlet name derives from the Spanish work Mata, meaning kill. Matanzas is therefore, the place of many slaughters."

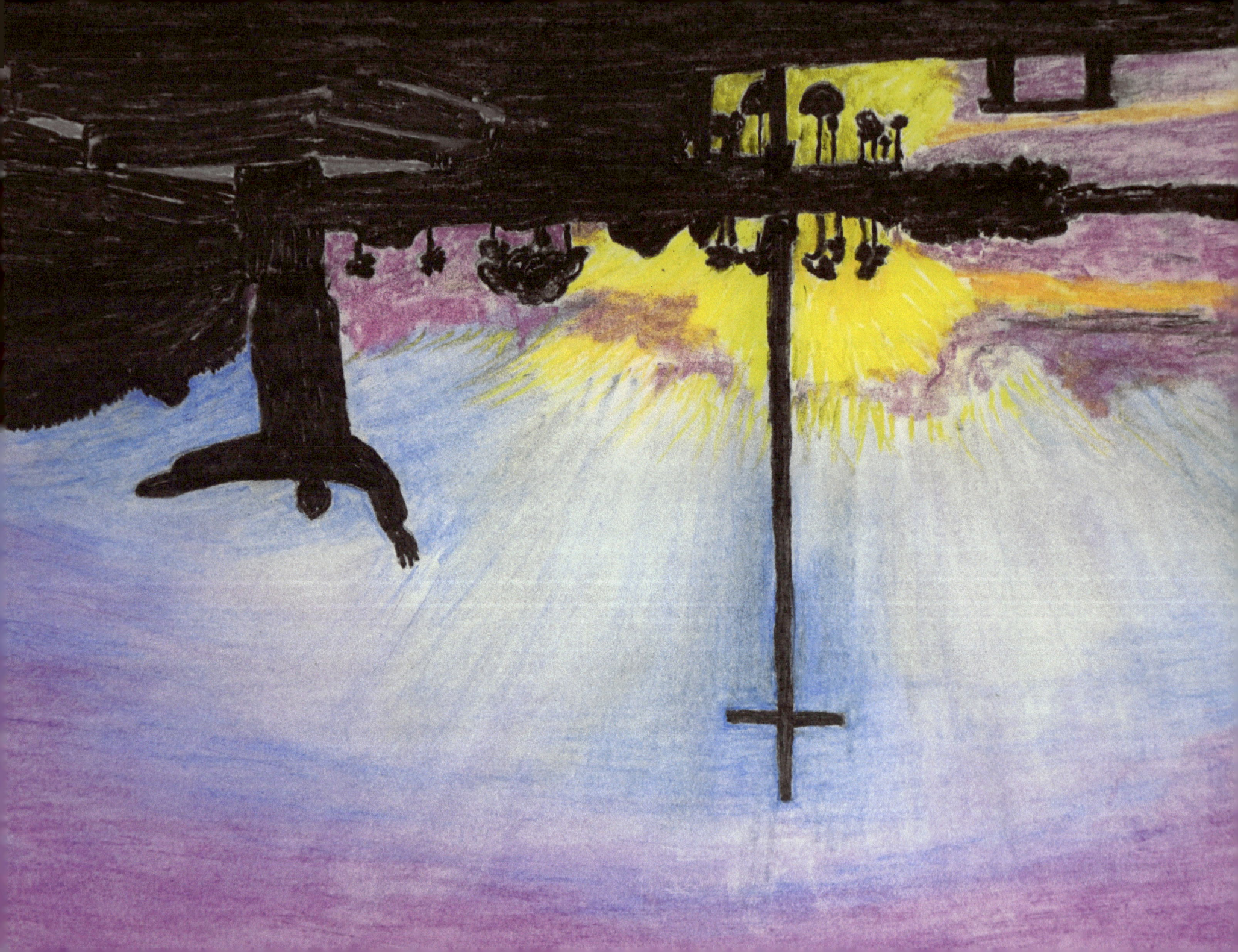

# The Great Cross and Father Francisco Lopez de Mendoza Grajales

When Menendez first landed on the beach, he placed a wooden cross in the sand and established the new colony of St Augustine on September 8, 1565.  Menendez' crew included four priests, with Father Francisco Lopez de Mendoza Grajales serving as chaplain.  After planting the cross, Father Lopez said mass in honor of the Nativity of the Blessed Mary, and the Spanish colonists and the local Timucua Indians shared a feast, the continent's first Thanksgiving.  The Spanish would have served a stew made from salted pork and garbanzo beans, laced with garlic, and accompanied by hard sea biscuits and red wine.  It is likely that the Timucuans would have contributed turkey, venison, gopher tortoise, mullet and other fish, corn, beans and squash. This thanksgiving meal was celebrated 56 years before the Puritan-Pilgrim thanksgiving at Plymouth Plantation.

The current 280-foot-tall cross was installed 400 years later to commemorate the city's founding by Menendez.  The bronze statue of Father Lopez was sculpted in 1962 by Ivan Mestrovic, the dean of art at the University of Notre Dame (our alma mater).

The initial Spanish settlement was built on the remains of an early Indian village, located on or near the site of the current Fountain of Youth Park.  This settlement was used for less than a year, then moved to Anastasia Island.  Due to erosion and military defenses the settlement was moved to the mainland in 1572, centered around the current Plaza de la Constitucion.

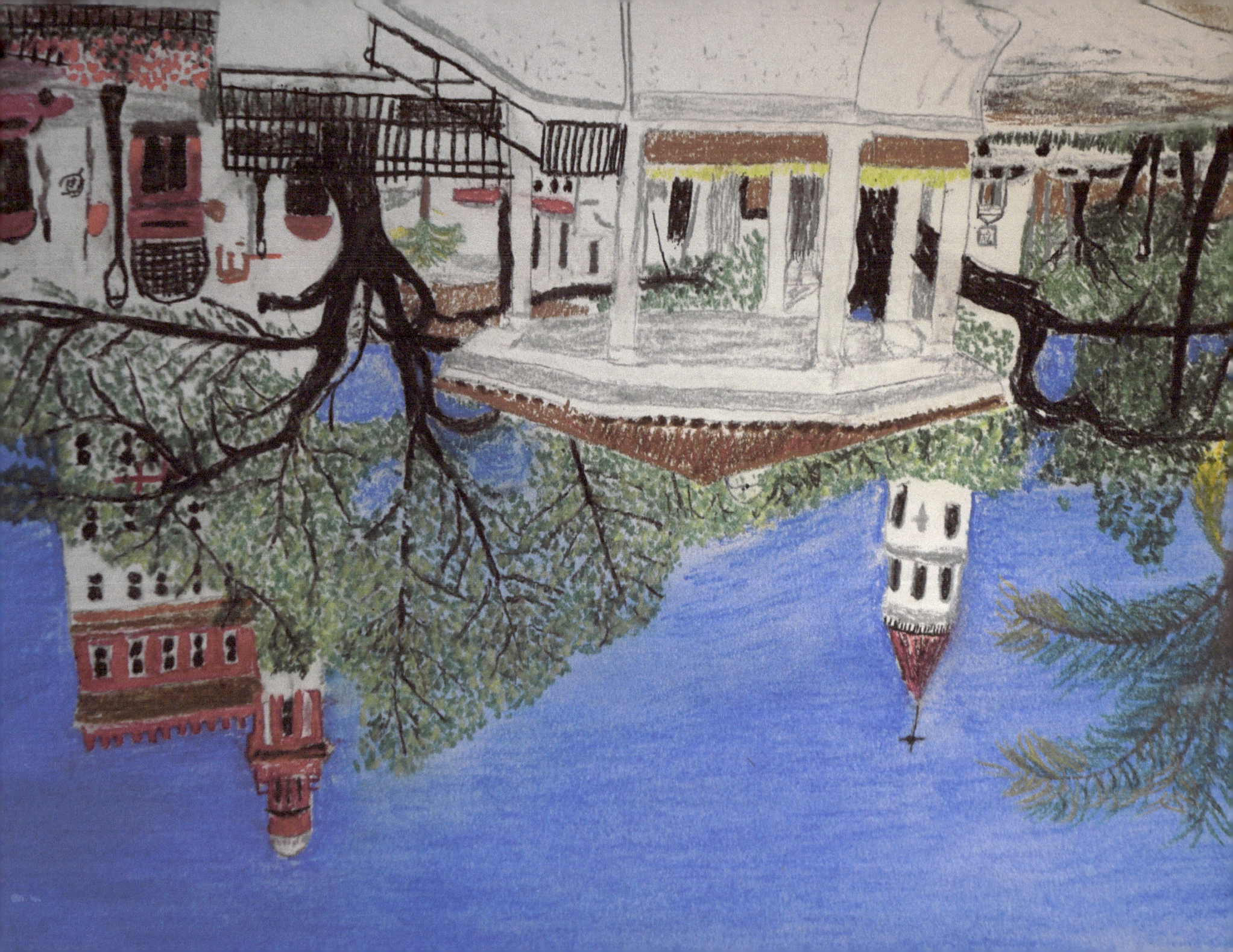

# Plaza de la Constitucion

The plaza is the oldest public park in the United States having been established by Spanish ordinances in 1573. The plaza is surrounded by surviving structures, such as the Government House and the Cathedral Basilica of St Augustine.

From the park emanate the city's oldest streets, such as Aviles Street and St. George Street, which are pedestrian friendly avenues for tourists to shop, dine and explore the buildings that span the 500 plus year history of the city.

In 1808, Napoleon invaded Spain, and overthrew the king. When Napoleon was defeated, Spain enacted their first written constitution. Spain directed that plazas throughout their empire be renamed. St Augustine's plaza was renamed Plaza de la Constitucion in commemoration of the event.

From the beginning, the plaza served as a center of commerce for the settlement. A popular event is the Colonial Night Watch in which citizens on the street after the gates were locked were required to carry a light for identification by the Night Watch. A torchlit parade of reenactors of British and Spanish soldiers, Native Americans, and Florida militia proceed from Castillo de San Marcos through the city gates to the Plaza.

The Plaza is the center of the Night of Lights, with millions of tiny white lights illuminating the ancient city.

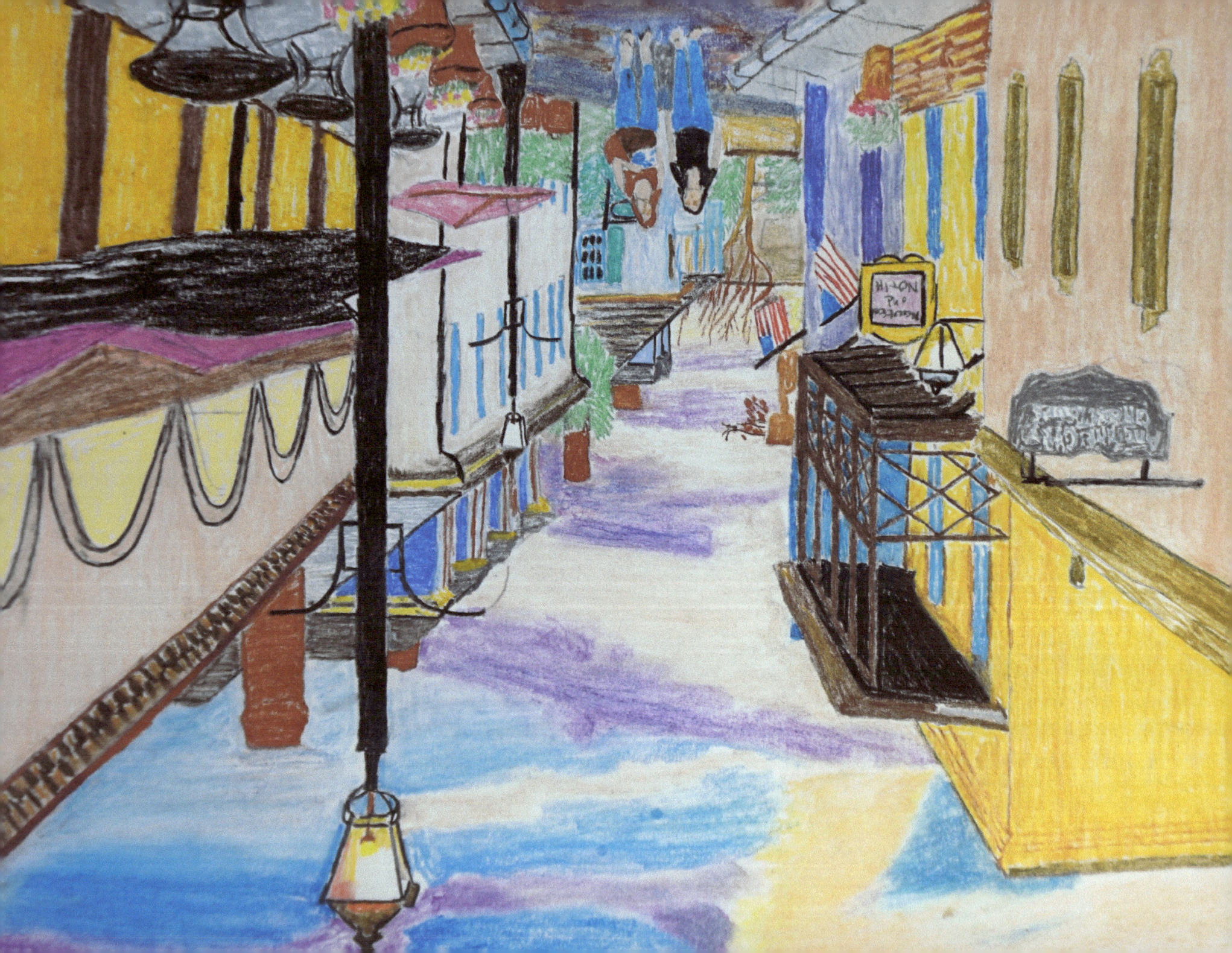

# Aviles Street

St. Augustine has the distinction of being the oldest city in America, having been established by Pedro Menendez de Aviles on September 8, 1565.  Aviles Street is considered to be the oldest city street in the country, having been listed on the city's oldest maps, from the 1570s.  It was originally named Hospital Street, as it was the location of the colony's military hospital.  It was later renamed Aviles Street after the city founder's hometown.

The first parish church, Nuestra de Los Remedios, (Our Lady of Remedies) was built near the corner of Aviles and King Streets.  Over the years it was destroyed by the pirate Francis Drake in 1586 and finally burned by British forces in 1702.

Today Aviles Street is a popular tourist destination, with art and craft galleries, numerous restaurants with outdoor seating, museums housed in some of the oldest houses in St Augustine and Bed and Breakfasts.

A wooden gateway arch at the corner of King Street supported by granite pillars marks the entrance to the historic street.

The General Kirby House is home to the St Augustine Historical Society with a collection of Florida history materials.  The Spanish Military Hospital Museum is a tribute to the early hospital from which the street got its first name.  The Antiques and Collectibles is located in the former city jail.

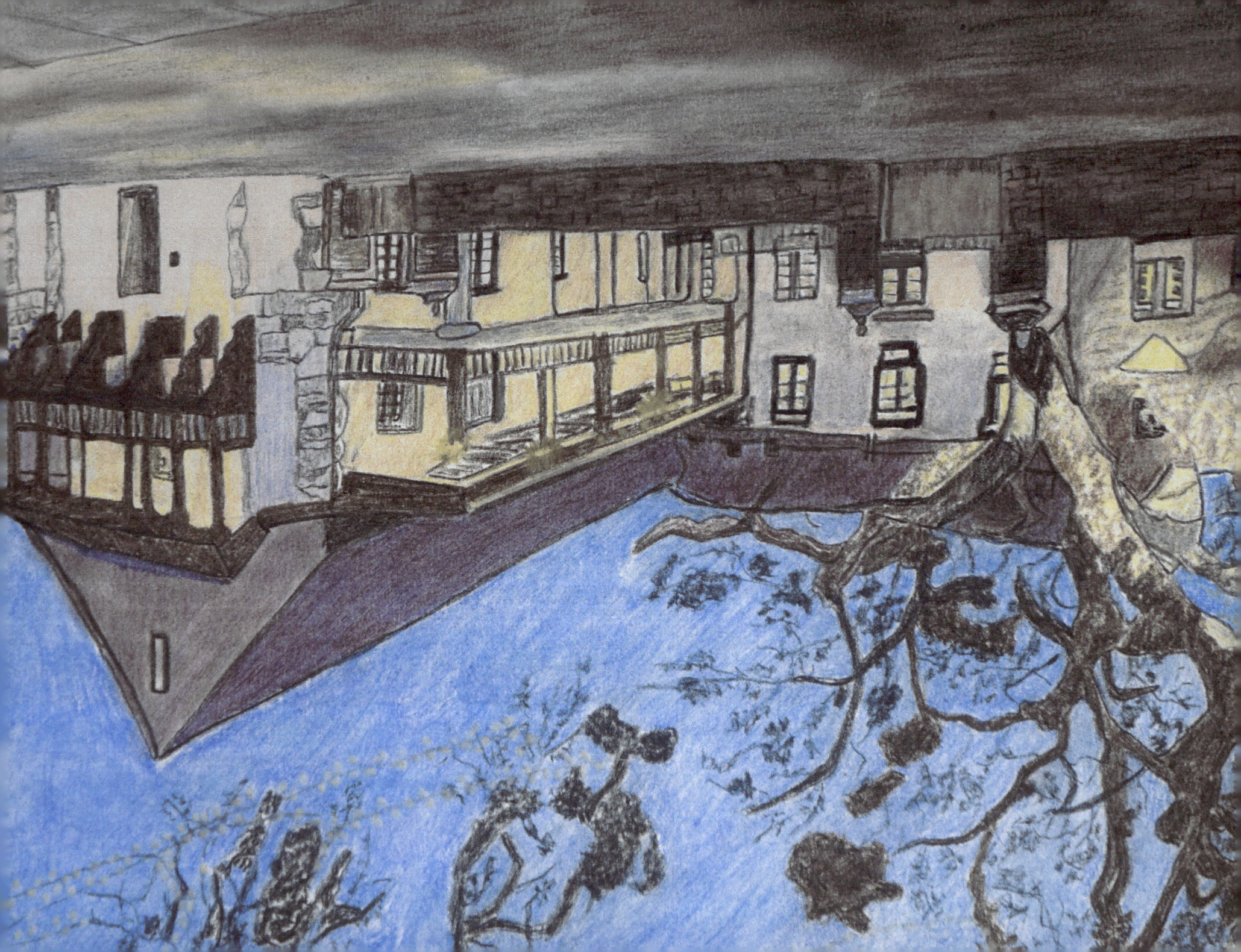

# Government House

Government House bounds the west side of the Plaza de la Constitucion. The building, constructed of coquina, was completed around 1710 and served as the residence for Spanish governors.

In 1754, the Seven Years War broke out in Europe. In North America, the war was known as the French and Indian War. St Augustine was not involved in the conflict, but when peace was made, Florida was turned over to Britain. On July 20, 1763, the British raised the Union Jack over the Castillo, renamed Fort St Marks, and the British governor occupied Government House. Most Spanish residents of St Augustine fled to Cuba.

The British split Florida into two colonies: East Florida with St Augustine as its capital; and West Florida governed from Pensacola. For 20 years East and West Florida stayed under British Rule. In 1778, Spain joined with the American rebels and in 1779, the Spanish fleet captured West Florida. When the war ended, East and West Florida were ceded back to Spain.

In the War of 1812, American militias invaded Florida, hoping to convince the population to proclaim independence from Spain. Various skirmishes followed, and in 1819, the Adams-Otis treaty was signed in which the Florida colonies were turned over to the United States, with Andrew Jackson serving as the military governor of the Territory of Florida.

Government House served as a military hospital during the Civil War. After the war, it served as a courthouse and customs house. It was expanded in 1937 and used by the US Postal Service. In 1964, it was transferred to the State of Florida, and houses a museum and serves as the headquarters of the state's local historical preservation effort.

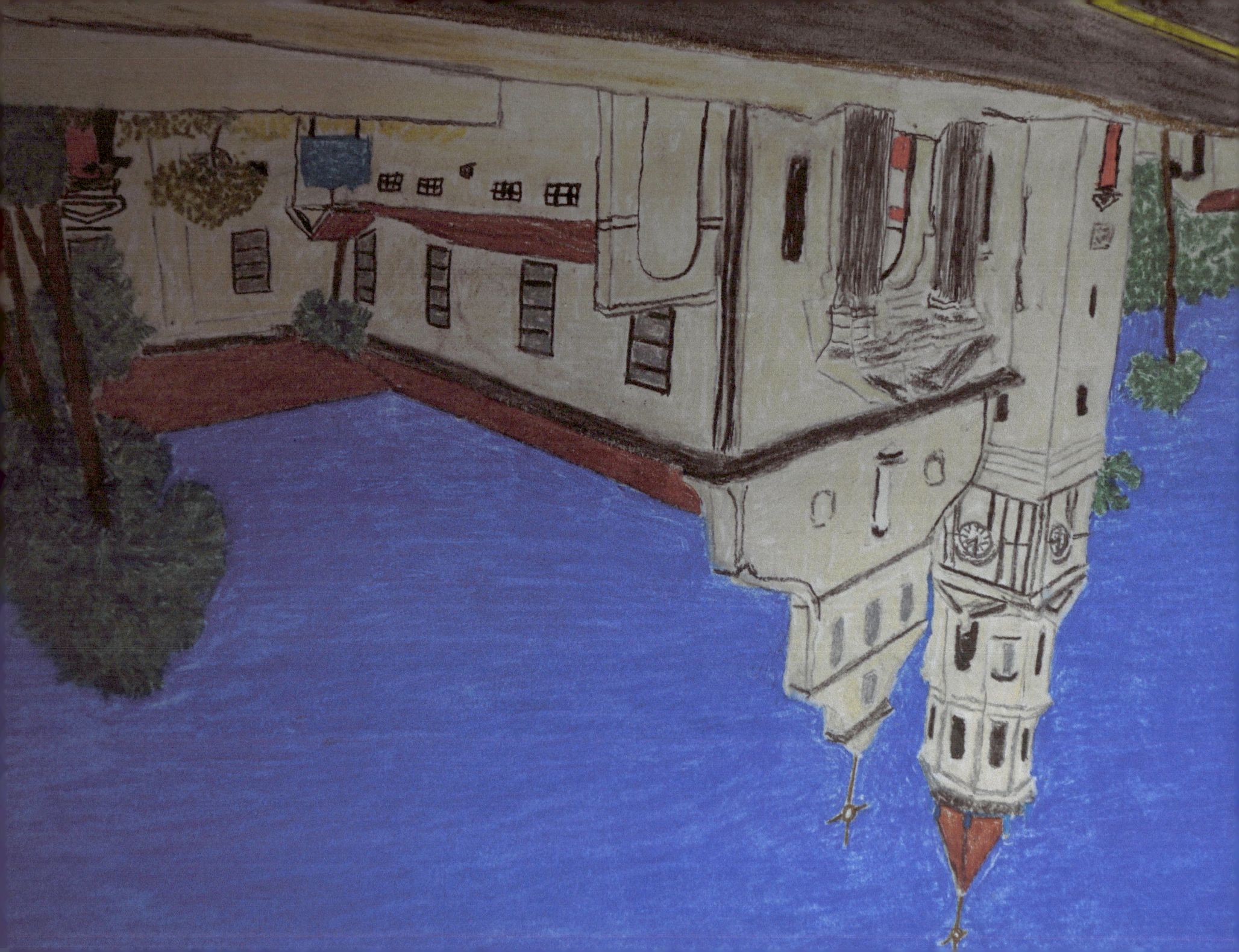

# St. Augustine Cathedral

St. Augustine's first Catholic Cathedral was relatively simple, and was soon burned by Sir Francis Drake. A second cathedral was built in a matter of months, using straw and Palmetto, and it too did not last long, being destroyed by fire in 1599. A third Cathedral was built of timber, which lasted 95 years. After this church was burned down in 1702, it was not replaced for over ninety years. During this time, Britain took over the colony.

When Spain regained control, plans for the Cathedral we know today were drawn up, locating it and an orange grove on the north side of Plaza de la Constitucion. Construction began in 1793, with walls made of coquina from Anastasia Island, and completed four years later.

In 1887, the cathedral burned, but the outer coquina walls were fireproof and survived. The church was rebuilt due to funds provided by Henry Flagler and the congregation. The church was enlarged, and reached its present form.

The St Augustine Cathedral stands today as Florida's last surviving Spanish Colonial church.

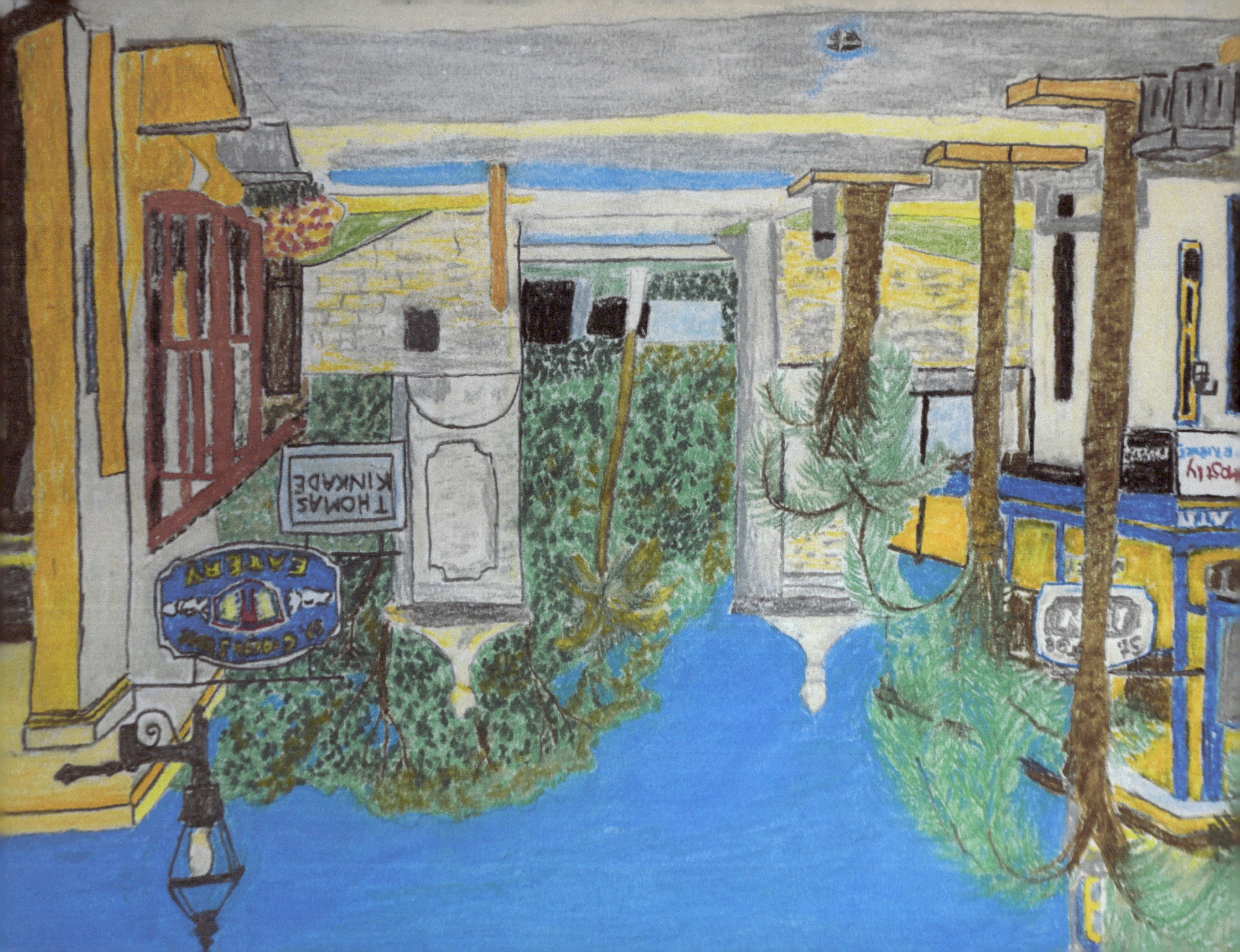

# St. George Street

In the early days of St Augustine, St George street was the main street. It is now a pedestrian only thoroughfare that is currently the heart of the city's historic district.   In 1704, a wall was built around the city, which was already 150 years old at the time. The gates and walls at the north end of St. George street, are some of what remains.

Heading south from the gates, one finds the oldest wooden schoolhouse in the United States.  Later on, the street stood an Old Grist Mill and once contained shops and a tavern that is being rebuilt.  Further along the street is the Colonial Quarter, a two-acre attraction that shows what life was like for many centuries in St. Augustine, including replicas of the forts and watchtower. The Colonial Oak is an area where concerts are held under a sweeping live oak. The Bull & Crown Public House is on the Colonial Quarter property.

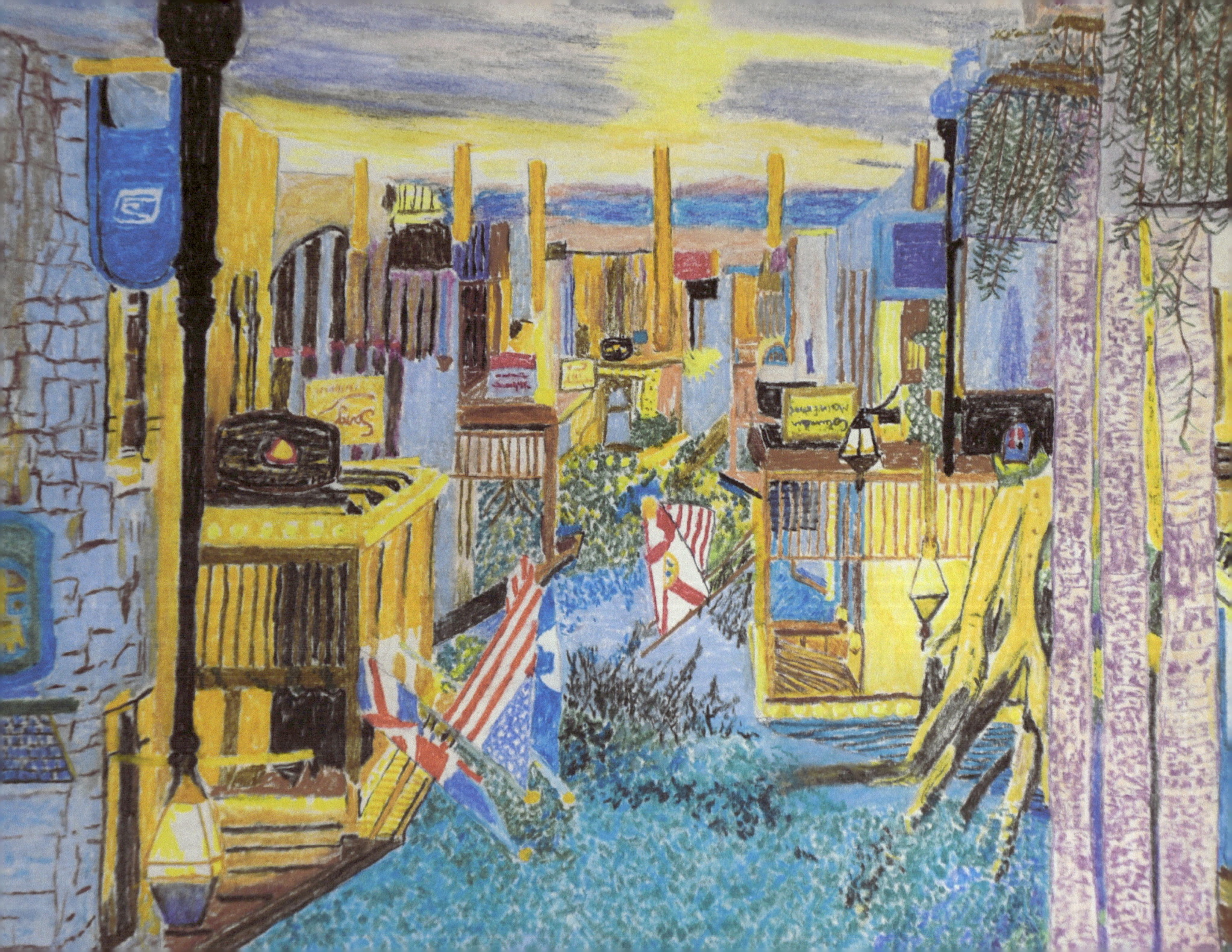

# St. George Street

Many shops and restaurants line St George Street and span out
on the streets that intersect it.

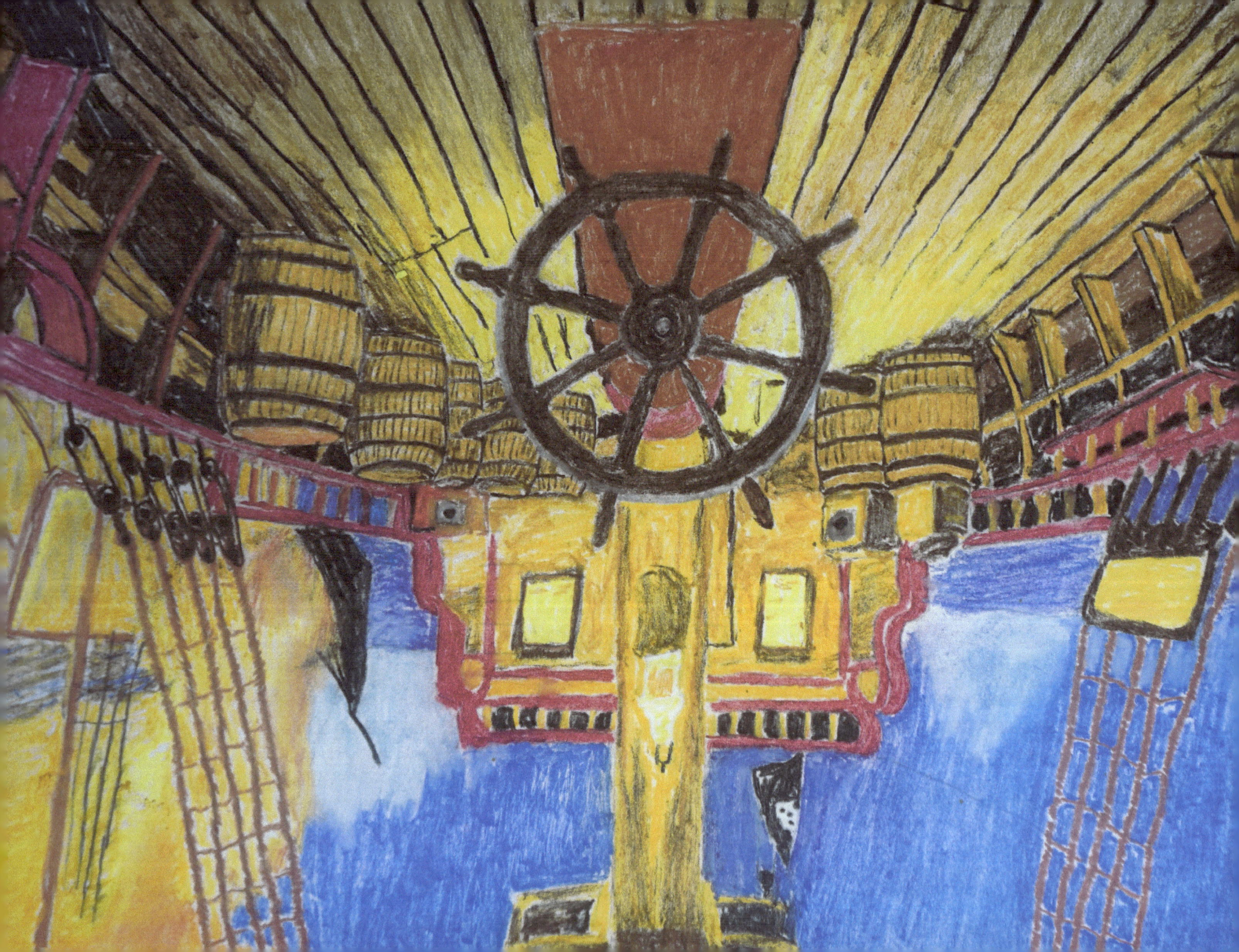

# The Pirate & Treasure Museum

Colonization of the New World produced vast treasures for Spain, most notably gold and silver, but also gems, pearls, spices, sugar, lumber and agricultural goods. Spain set up a convoy route in the 1560s, that passed between Cuba and La Florida, using the gulf stream to assist in crossing the Atlantic. This flow of treasures made Spain the richest country in Europe by the end of the 16th century.

These treasures were the envy of the other countries of Europe, notably England and France. They did not dare to take on the Spanish directly, having lost the 65-year war. They resorted to privateers to raid the Spanish Colonies and fleets. Privateers were private warships who were authorized by England and France to raid Spanish colonies and treasure fleets and shared their plunder.

On June 7, 1586, Sir Francis Drake, the English Privateer and a force of 2,000 men and more than forty ships, arrived. St Augustine's governor Pedro Menendez Marquez (nephew of Pedro Menendez de Aviles) evacuated the city's women and children and moved the city's treasures to the new wooden fort, still under construction. Drake's forces brought artillery to bear on the new fort, and Menendez, who realized that he could not defend the fort, escaped.

When some of the Spanish soldiers clashed with Drake's men, wounding a few, Drake retaliated by ordering his men to burn the city and raze the fort. Following this raid, Menendez convinced King Philip II of Spain to rebuild the town with a new wooden fortress and increase the number of soldiers defending it. The new fort was named Castillo de San Marcos, the same name as the stone fortress built a century later.

Following this raid, Menendez convinced King Philip II of Spain to rebuild the town with a new wooden fortress and increase the number of soldiers defending it. The new fort was named Castillo de San Marcos, the same name as the stone fortress built a century later.

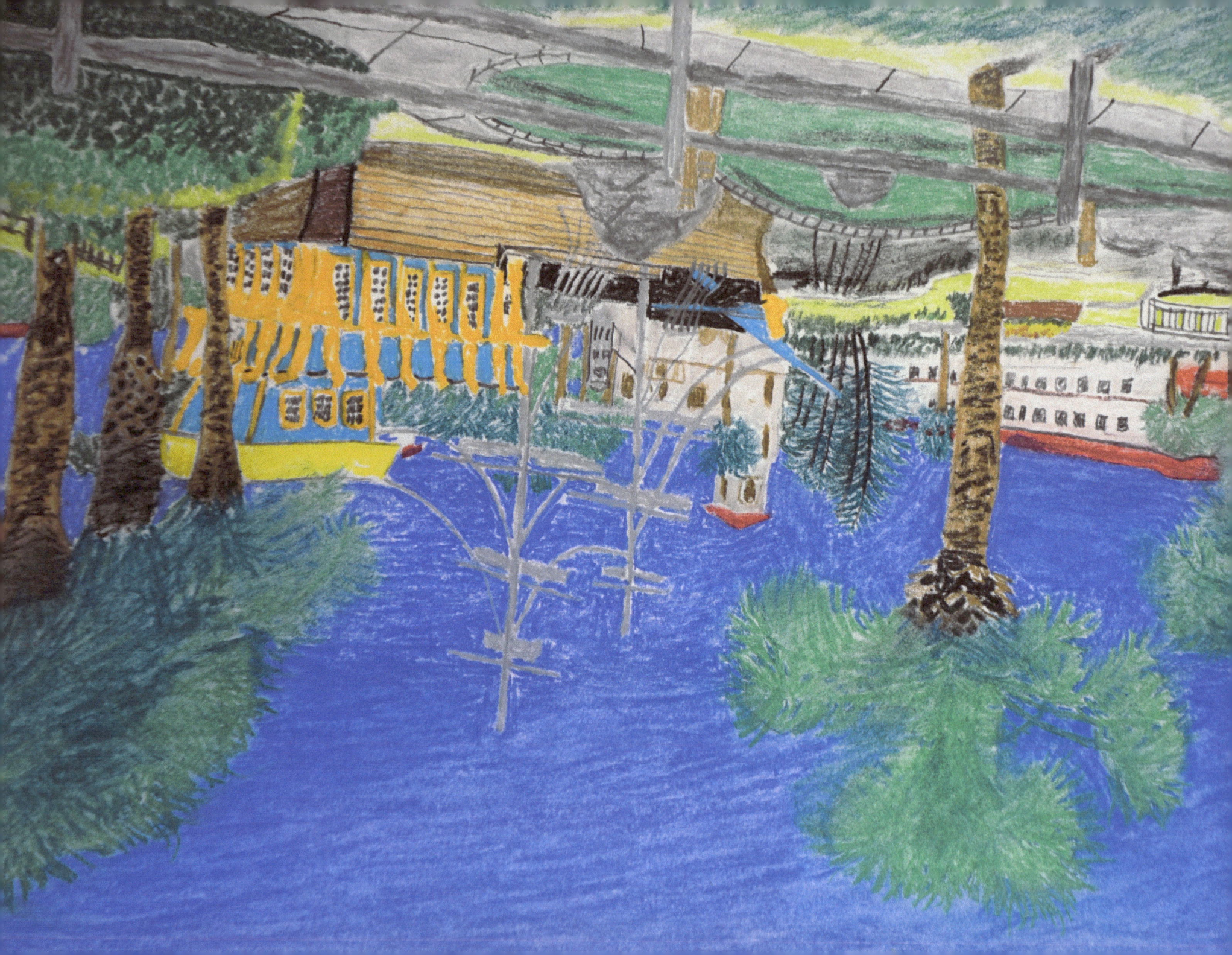

## Pirate Themed Miniature Golf at St. Augustine Beach

Present day St. Augustine celebrates the lighter side of pirates, with an annual Pirate festival at Francis Field, where celebrants dress up as pirates and wenches. At parades for Christmas, St Patrick's Day and Easter, there are usually a few pirate ship floats to provide local flavor to the event.

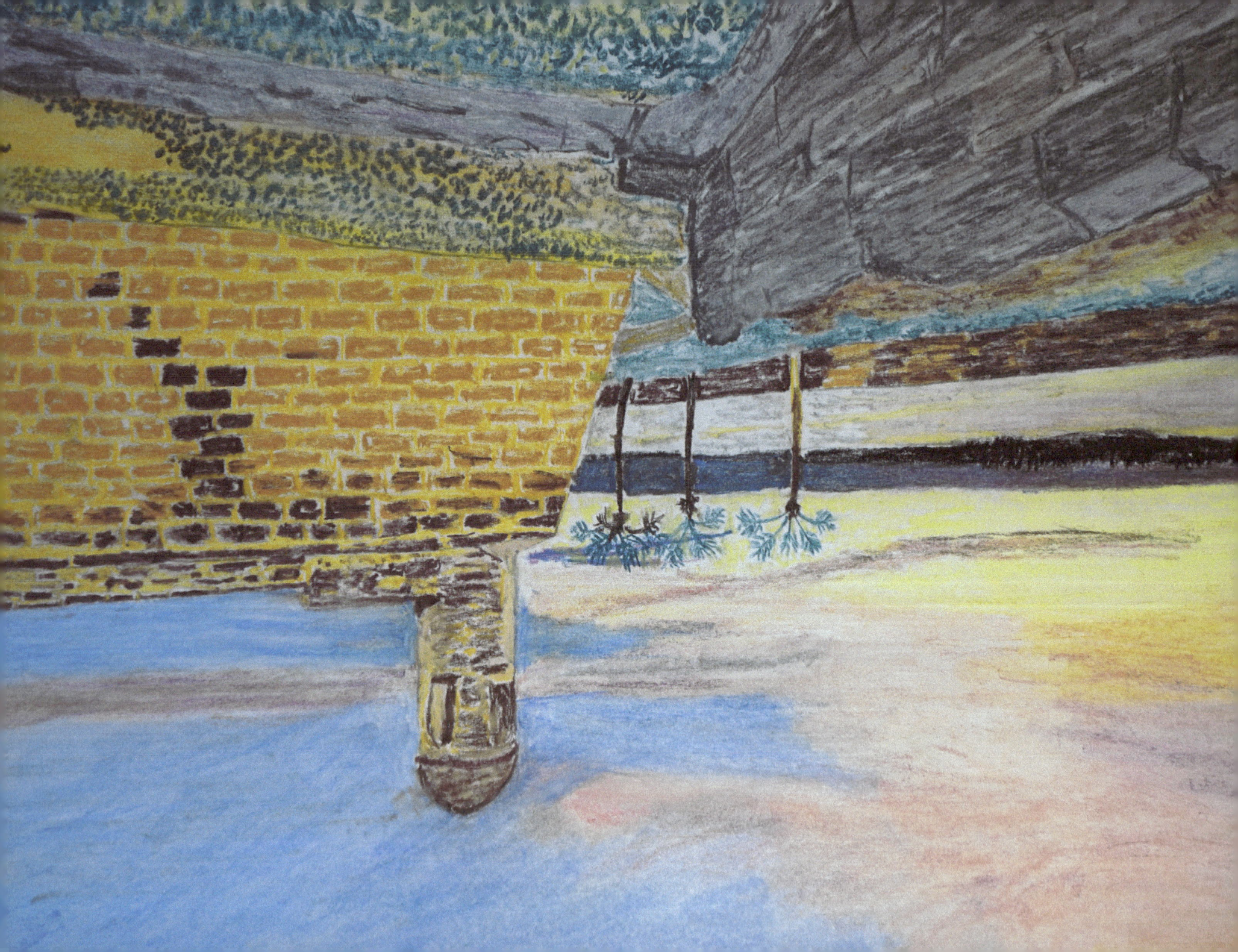

# Castillo de San Marcos

While there were many pirates and privateers plying the waters off the coast of Florida, they preyed on ships and did not attack St Augustine for four decades after Drake's raid. Then on May 29, 1688, the English Privateer Robert Searles sacked the city, killed residents and took Africans and Indians to be sold as slaves.

In response to this raid, the Spanish Crown ordered the reorganization of Florida's militia and construction of a stone fortress to guard the city. Construction commenced in 1672 and was completed in 1695.

The fort was constructed of coquina, quarried from Anastasia Island. Coquina was formed by the deposition of tiny coquina clam shells that accumulated in the shallow waters of Florida. Over time, acid rain dissolved some of the calcium and formed calcium carbonate, cementing the shells into a porous limestone. When wet, coquina was soft and easily cut into blocks. When dried, the rock hardened, but retained its porous structure. Oyster shells were burned to form lime, which was mixed with sand to use as a mortar for cementing the coquina blocks.

Later repairs were made with Portland cement, which caused the coquina to become brittle and failed. Currently the Portland cement is being replaced with a mixture based on the original lime mortar.

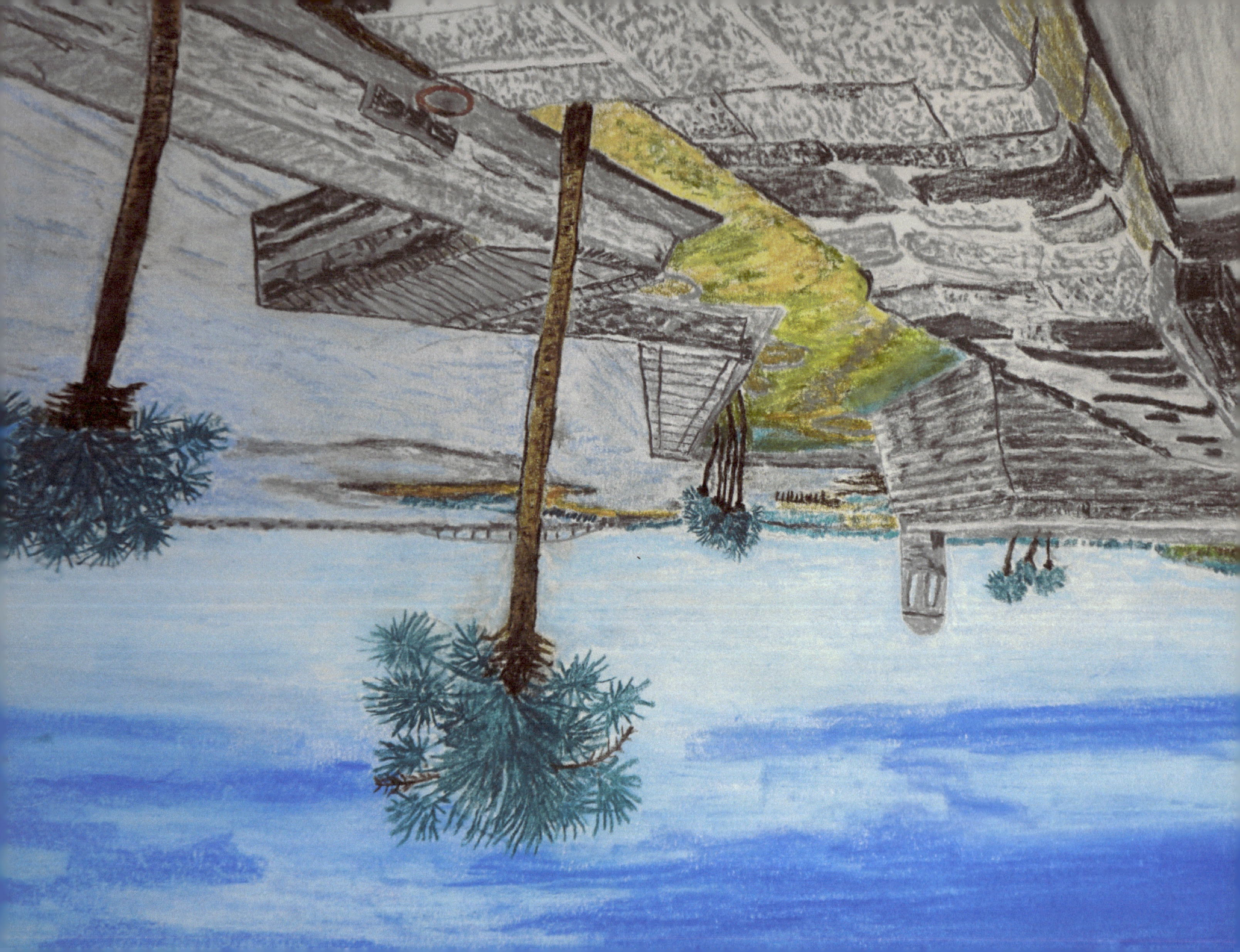

# Castillo de San Marcos

The coquina turned out to be very effective in resisting attack. When James Moore, the English Governor of Charleston led an attack of the fort, they could not damage its walls.

The story is that the cannon balls embedded themselves in the coquina walls. The defenders went out at night to pry the cannon balls from the coquina, then fired them back at the English ships the next day.

The fort withstood a 27-day siege by General Oglethorpe in 1740. Unlike the earlier wooden forts, that were repeatedly burned, the coquina Castillo was never taken by force. Spain was defeated by Britain in the Seven Year War, and in 1763, turned over Florida. The fort was re-named Fort Mark, and St Augustine became capital of East Florida. Britain returned Florida to Spain in 1783 following the defeat of the British in the American Revolutionary War. In 1819, Spain ceded Florida to the United States. The fort was again renamed, Fort Marion. During the Civil War, the fort was under the confederacy. All told, the Fort changed hands six times, all peacefully.

In 1933, the fort was taken over by the National Park Service, and renamed Castillo de San Marcos, to honor its Spanish Heritage.

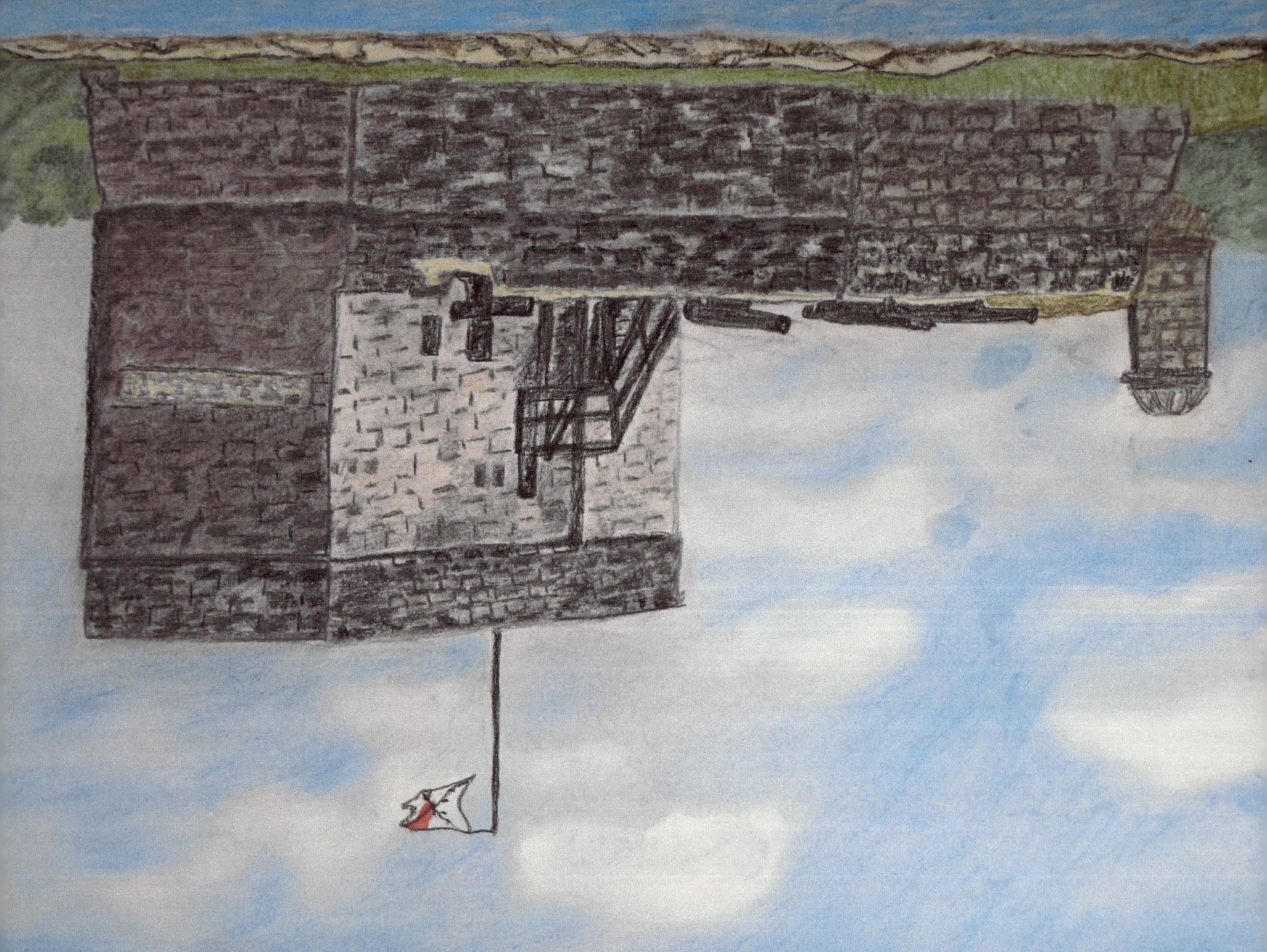

# Fort Matanzas

The Spanish placed a series of watch towers at the Matanzas inlet to protect the southern approaches to St Augustine.  The current fort was completed in 1742, to serve as protection of the southern entrance to the city.  Fort Matanzas was constructed of coquina, like Castillo de San Marcos.

Designed for up to 50 soldiers, it was lightly defended. In 1742, as the fort was nearing completion, the British approached the inlet with twelve ships. Cannon fire drove off the scouting boats, and the warships left without engaging the fort. This was the only time the fort fired on an enemy.

The Spanish did not maintain the fort, and it fell in ruin after the United States took over Florida.  After the fort walls were stabilized, the National Park Service took over the fort and operates it as a tourist attraction, served by a ferry boats from South Anastasia Island.

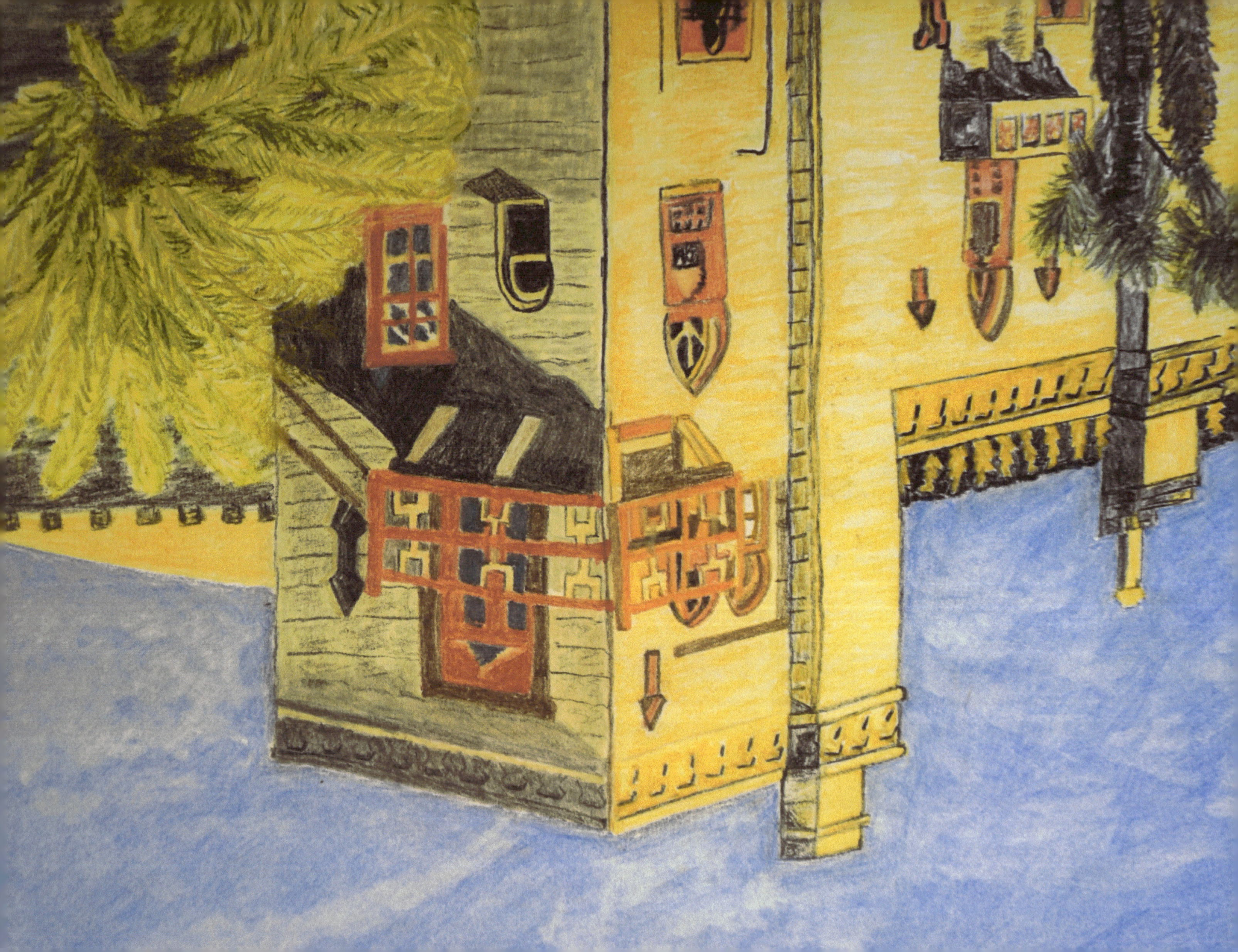

# Villa Zorayda

Villa Zorayda was built in 1883 by Boston millionaire, Franklin W Smith as his winter home. It was inspired by the 12th century Moorish Alhambra Palace in Granada, Spain. It was the first building constructed of formed concrete in Florida. It used an aggregate of crushed coquina shells.

Smith encouraged Henry Flagler to move to St. Augustine and invest in the city. Villa Zorayda is across the street from Flagler's hotels, the Ponce de Leon and the Alcazar, and a block from the Casa Monica that Smith built, then sold to Flagler.

In addition to its intended purpose as a private residence, the Villa Zorayda has been used as a restaurant, a nightclub and gambling casino, and a hotel. The building underwent renovations beginning in 2003 and reopened to the public in 2008 as a museum.

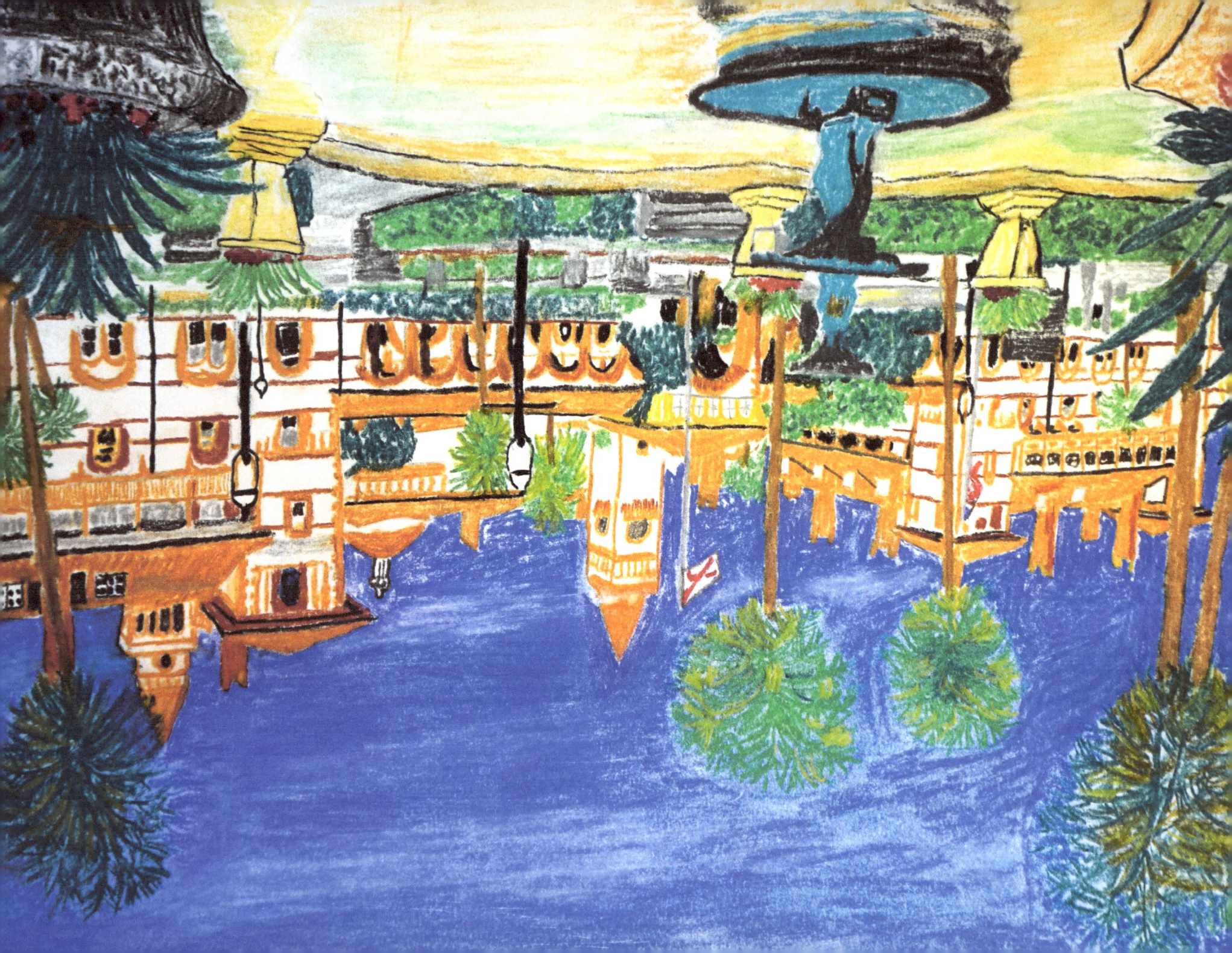

# Ponce de Leon Hotel (Flagler College)

Henry Flagler was a partner with John D. and William Rockefeller in forming the Standard Oil Company, which made him one of the richest men in America. Hoping to find a cure for his ailing wife, he took her to Florida. His wife died but he decided to invest in St Augustine, filling in a creek, and constructed his first hotel.

The 450-room Ponce de Leon Hotel was the first hotel constructed of reinforced concrete, with Portland cement and crushed coquina aggregate.

Construction of the Hotel was started on December 1, 1885. By the time it was finished, Flagler had spent $2.5 million. The hotel was lavishly decorated, with Louis Comfort Tiffany supplying stained glass windows and interior decoration. Thomas Alva Edison set up an electrical system, the first hotel to have electric lights. Electric lighting was so new, the guests feared it and did not know how to operate the new switches, so Edison had staff go around to the rooms to turn the lights on and off. Flagler welcomed the first guests on January 12, 1888.

To accommodate wealthy visitors from Ney York, Flagler bought a rail line from Jacksonville, which he converted to standard gauge and connected to rail lines from the north. The hotel did not operate like other s, renting rooms by the night. Prospective snow birds needed to reserve and pay for rooms for the entire winter season.

The hotel served as the flagship hotel in the Flagler empire. He eventually extended the railroad to Key West, adding a series of hotels along the way. He died in 1913, a year after his railroad reached Key West. In 1968, The Ponce de Leon Hotel became the main building of the newly founded Flagler College.

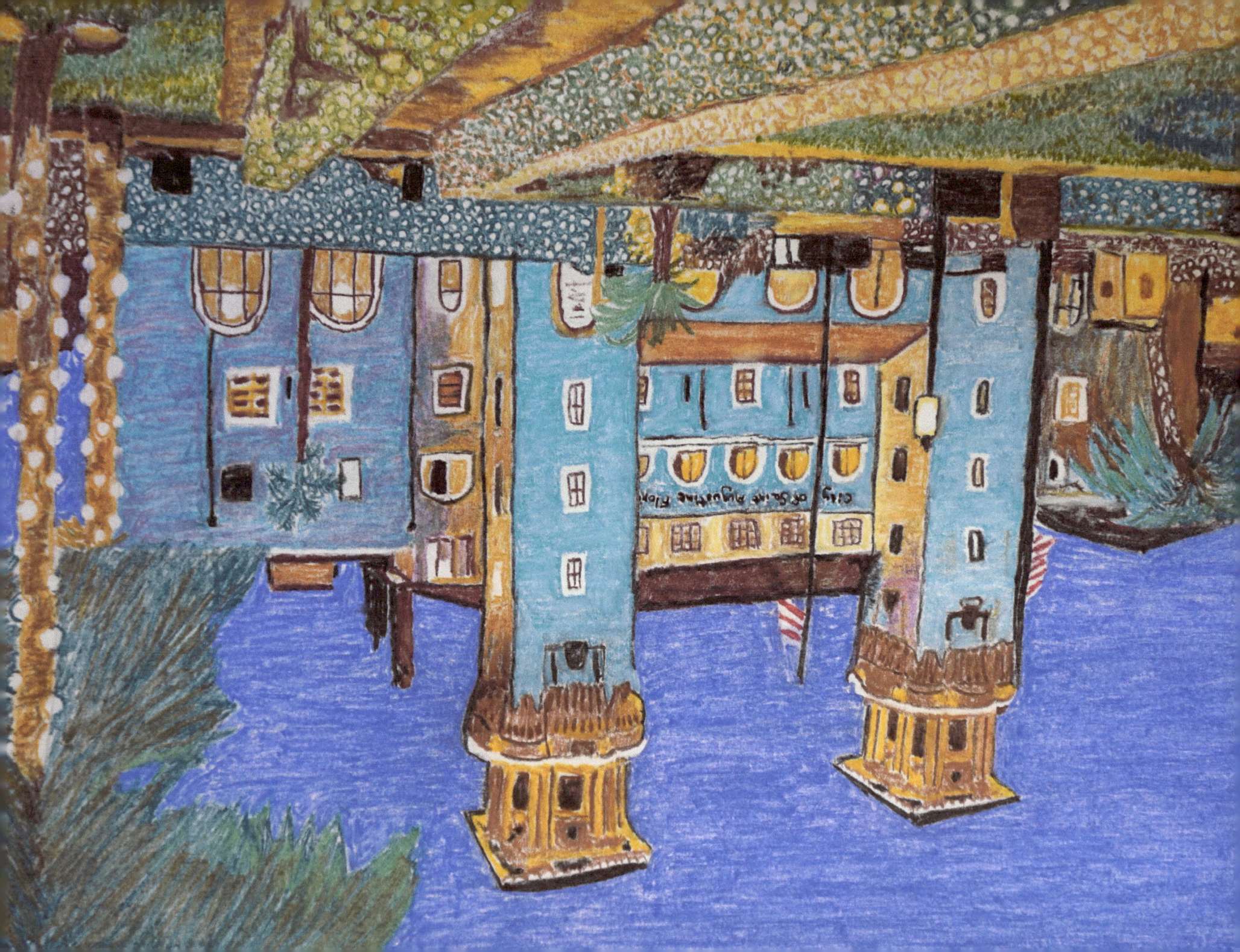

# Hotel Alcazar (Lightner Museum and City Hall)

Even before it formally opened, the Hotel Ponce de Leon was successful with advanced bookings. Flagler began construction of a second hotel in May 1987, across the street from the Ponce would be less expensive and less formal than the Ponce.

The Alcazar opened on Christmas Day, 1889. Its name is Arabic for "royal castle." The outer walls of the hotel were coquina. The four-story building was made of reinforced concrete, same as the Ponce. The hotel's original 300 rooms were eventually reduced to 170 when individual bathrooms were provided.

The southern section of the hotel (the Casino) had the nation's largest indoor swimming pool, with depths ranging from 4 feet to 14 feet. The pool was surrounded by a ballroom topped off with a glass roof. Near the pool were Turkish and Russian baths, and Swedish massage services. An artesian well supplied water which, like the Fountain of Youth, was presumed to have medicinal benefits. Tennis courts hosted then national tennis champions.

The Alcazar closed in 1930, a casualty of the Depression. It remained closed until Otto C. Lightner purchased it in 1947, renovated the Casino for some $150,000, and moved his collection of furniture, architectural fragments, mechanical musical instruments, natural history, fine arts, ceramics, glass and toys from Chicago to the new Lightner Museum. Lightner donated the building to the city of St Augustine, which occupies the rest of the building as City Hall since the 1970s.

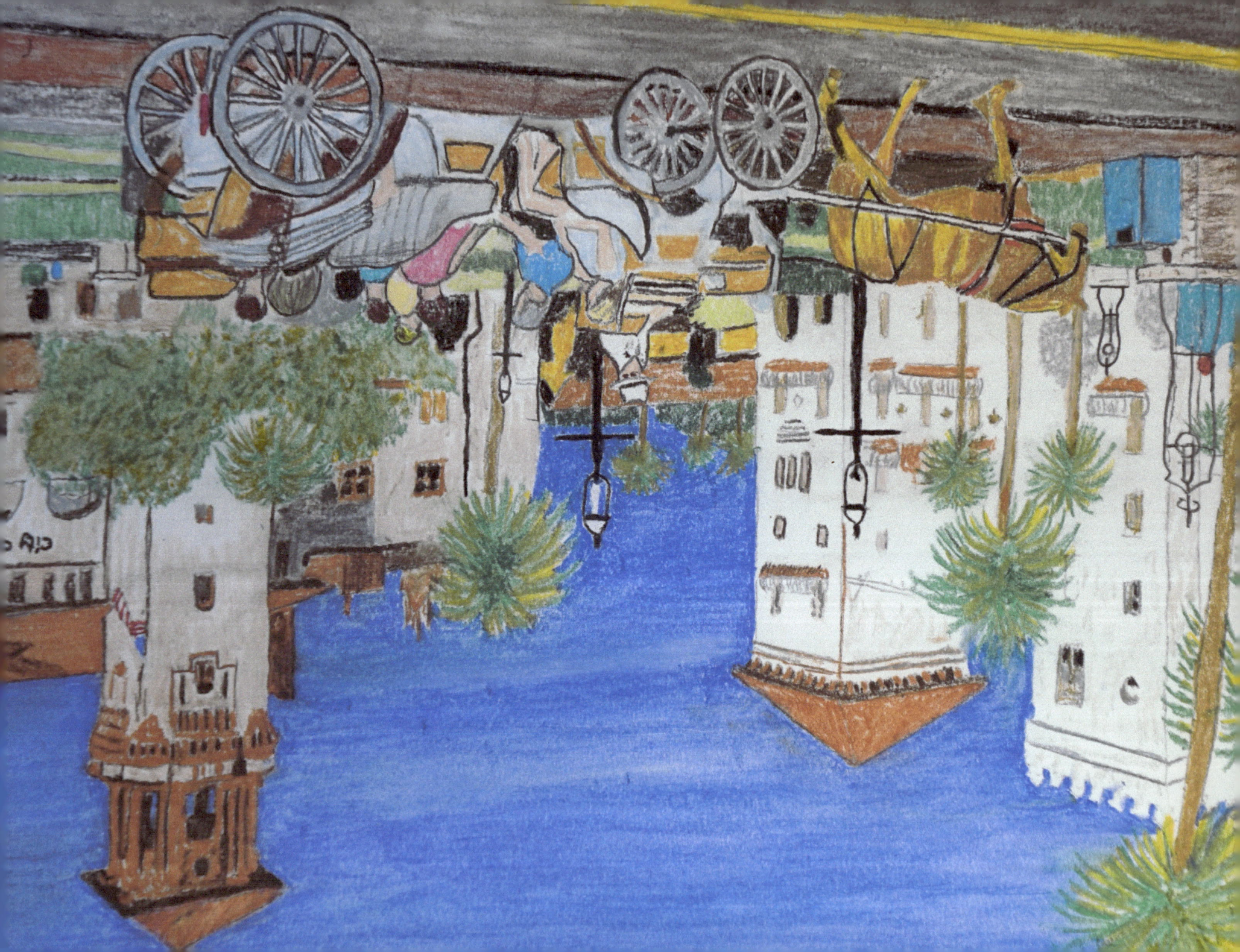

# Casa Monica Hotel

Franklin W Smith originally was given the chance to invest in
Flagler's new hotels. Instead he built a hotel across the street
from the Alcazar and the opposite corner from the Ponce.  The
Casa Monica (Spanish for "charming house") Hotel opened in
1988. As the story goes, Smith depended on Flagler's railroad to
transport finishing materials and furniture to the new hotel,
which caused delays in opening, resulting in financial problems
to Smith.

Four months after opening, the hotel was sold to Henry Flagler
who renamed it the Hotel Cordova.  Flagler then controlled the
three major hotels in St Augustine.

The Cordova operated until 1932, a victim of the Depression.  St
John's County purchased the former hotel in 1961 and
converted it to a courthouse.  In 1997, Richard Kessler
purchased the property, renovated it and reopened it under its
original name, the Casa Monica Hotel.

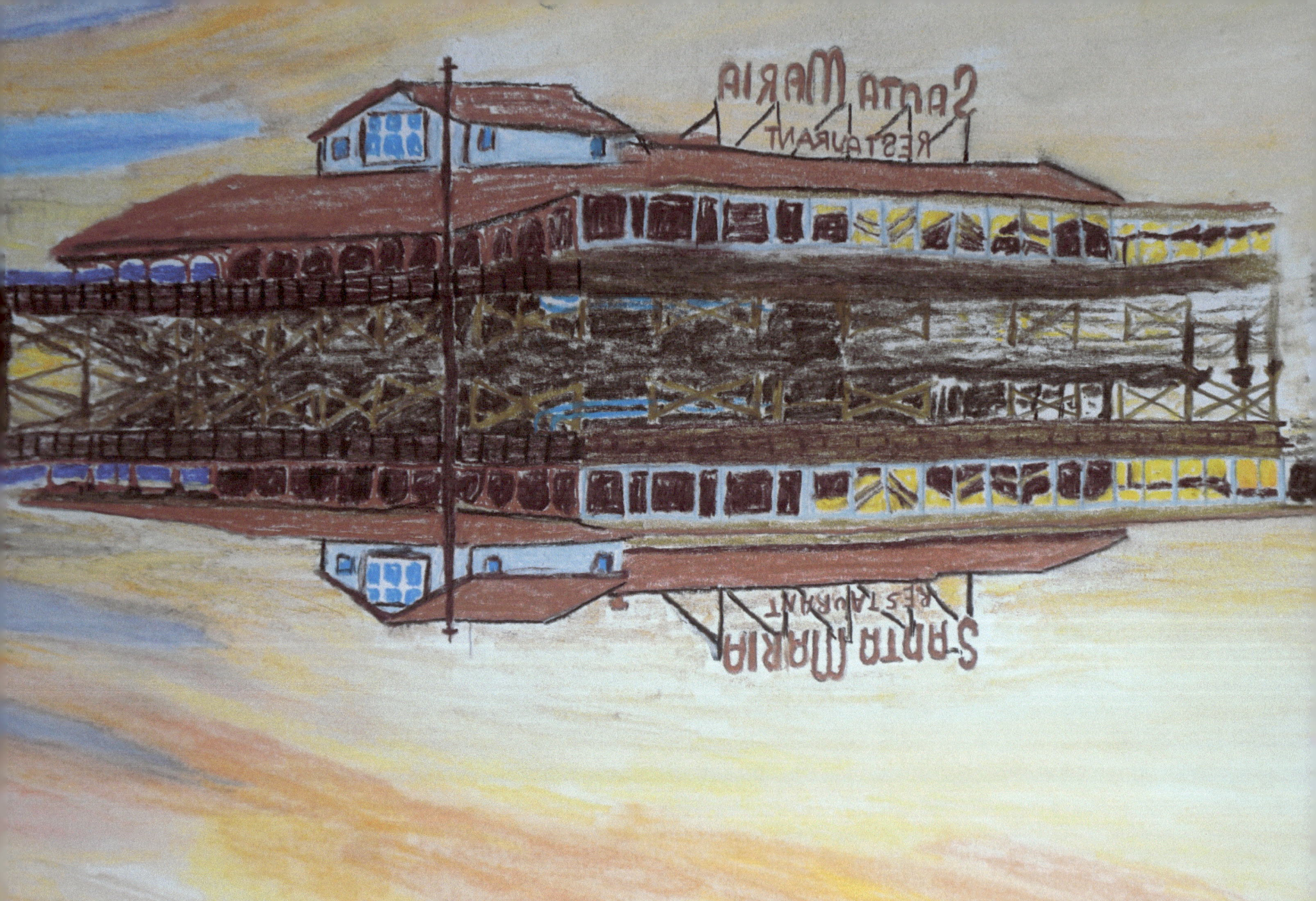

## Santa Maria Restaurant

This historic structure started in the 1930s as Corbett's Fish & Oyster Depot. The current building started as a series of smaller buildings that eventually merged together.

The Connell family started The Old Spanish Landing Restaurant in 1949. They changed the name to Santa Maria when they allowed a replica of the famous ship to be docked there as a tourist attraction.

The Santa Maria closed on March 26, 2015. David White of O.C. White's Seafood and Spirits purchased the building and business from the Connell family, and is planning a new two-story restaurant at the location.

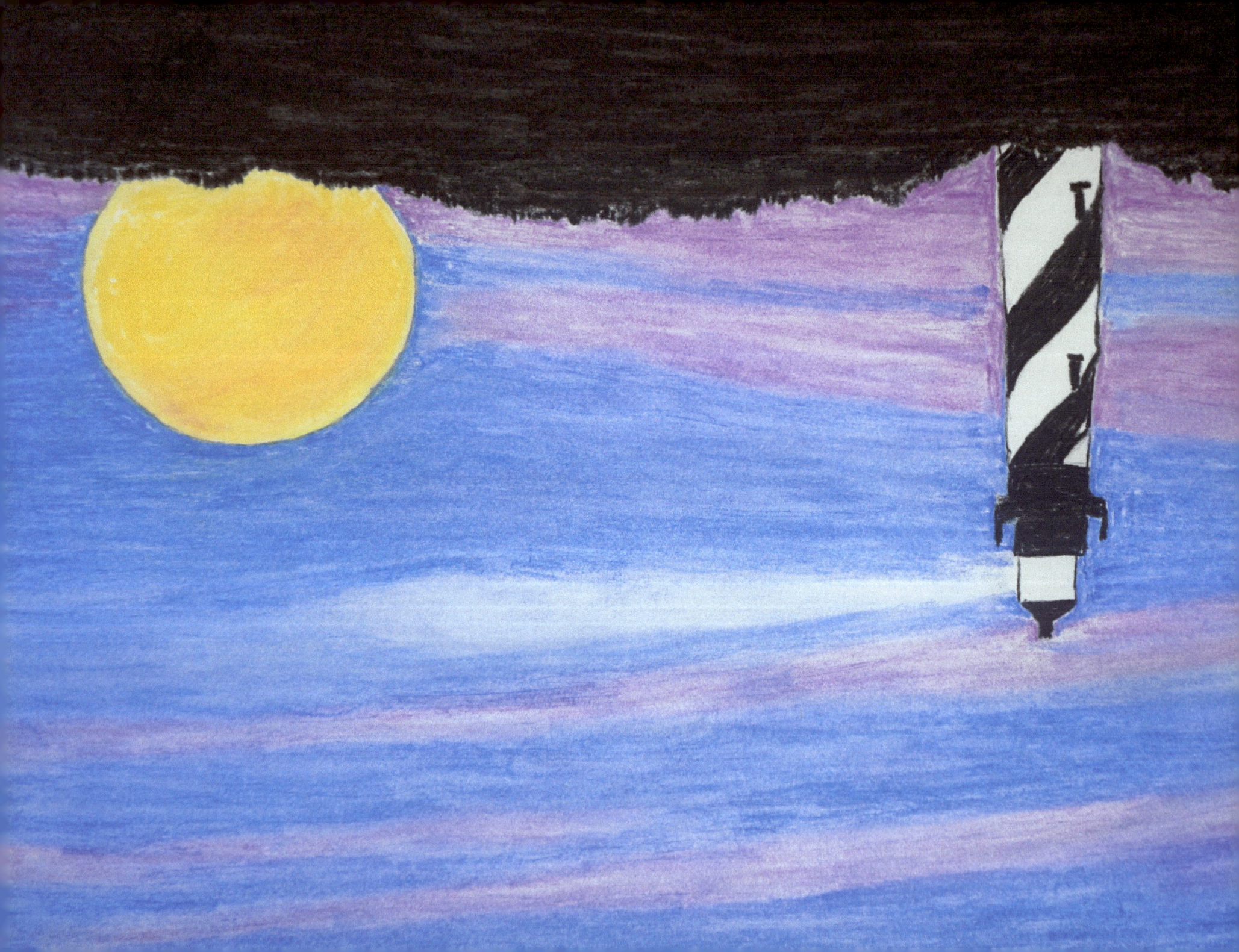

# St. Augustine Lighthouse

The St. Augustine lighthouse was the first established in the new territory of Florida in 1824.  It is reported to have been placed on the site of an earlier wooden watchtower, built by the Spanish in the 16th century.  In 1737, a more permanent coquina tower was built.  In 1783, during the 2nd Spanish rule, the lighthouse was improved.  Early lamps burned lard oil.

Beach erosion threatened the lighthouse, and a new one was completed in 1874, before the old one crashed into the sea in 1880. The light was electrified in 1936 and automated in 1955. In 1986, the lens to the light was damaged in a fire.  The antique lens was restored.  The lighthouse and surrounding buildings are managed by the St Augustine Lighthouse and Maritime Museum.

The lighthouse is the subject of numerous ghost stories.  The lighthouse has been featured in episodes of the SYFY series Ghost Hunters, and the program Ghost Story.   The St. Augustine Lighthouse & Maritime Museum offers tickets for a number of "Dark of the Moon" ghost tours.

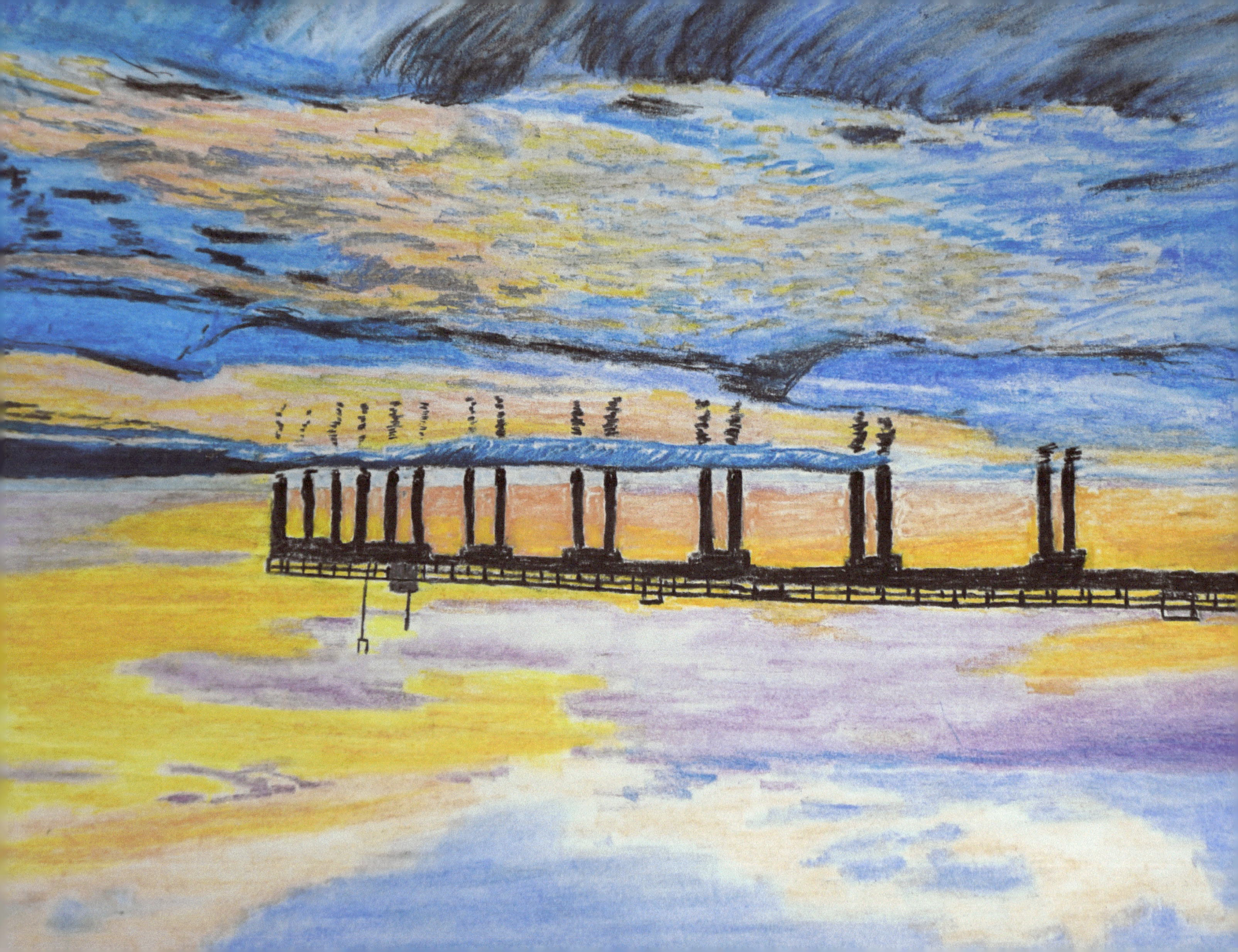

# Sunrise at the Saint Augustine Beach Fishing Pier

Anastasia Island was always a part of St. Augustine history. For a time, a settlement was made on the island before returning to the mainland. In the 19th century beach lovers would cross Matanzas Bay in sailboats, but the ocean side beaches were inaccessible across the marshes.

To make it easier to get to the beach (then called South Beach), a horse drawn railway was built to the beach which rode on wooden rails on a narrow causeway. In 1895, a wooden bridge was built from St Augustine to Anastasia Island. The bridge carried the South Beach Railway, with a steam locomotive and two small cars. Later the railway was replaced by a trolley car which went as far as A street in current St Augustine Beach.

St. Augustine Beach was founded just prior to World War I, as a summer resort. It was known variously as Chautauqua Beach and Assembly Beach.

When the trolley ceased operation in 1930, swimmers abandoned South Beach for Anastasia Beach (now Lighthouse Park) and installed a fishing pier. South Beach added a fishing pier and bath houses for changing to attract visitors back.

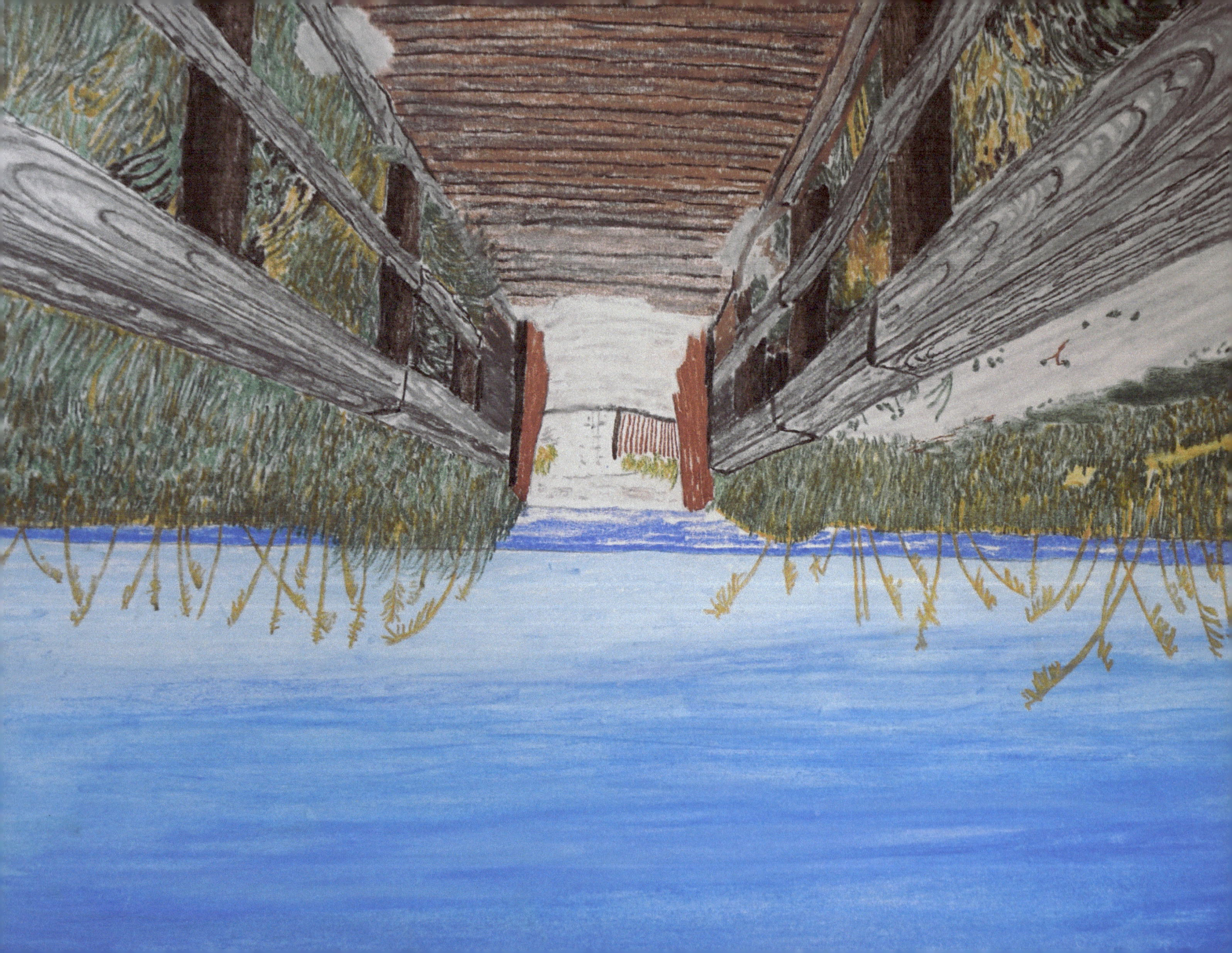

# Anastasia Island Beaches

Anastasia Island is 14 miles long and averages 1 mile in width, stretching from the St. Augustine Inlet to the Matanzas Inlet. The Island boasts a long coastline that is known for its soft white beaches, enjoyed by the residents of the island communities of St. Augustine Beach, Coquina Gables, Butler Beach, Crescent Beach, and Treasure Beach.

The island white sand is soft above the tidal area and is packed firmly by the waves below the high tide mark, making it easy to walk on or bicycle. The beach is accessible by 4-wheel drive vehicles who pay a toll during the summer. The tolls are used to support efforts to protect sea turtle nests, where the endangered Leatherback, Loggerhead and Green turtles come ashore to nest and lay their eggs from June through late September.

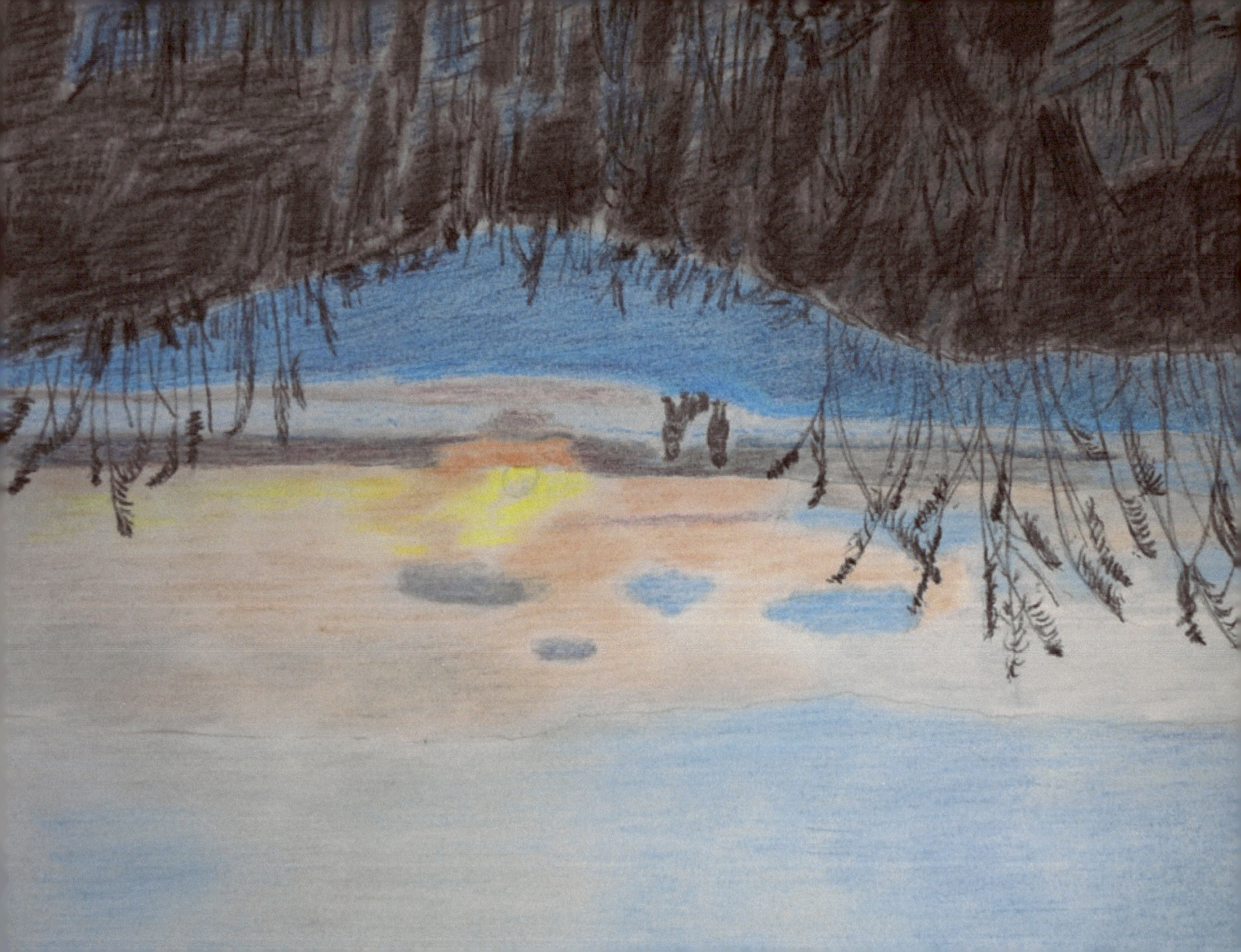

# Anastasia Island Dunes

In the early days after the bridge brought cars to the island, the hard-packed sands were used to race cars, when not bringing sunbathers from the city to the beaches. Waves and wind are constantly rearranging the soft white sand.  Sea Oats grow on the moving sand, trapping sand and forming dunes.

The sea oat roots strengthen the dunes which protect the island from winter Nor'easters, and the occasional hurricane.  At the northern end of St. Augustine Beach and communities north of the St. Augustine inlet, development took place on the dunes. This development along with routine dredging of the St Augustine inlet, has contributed to severe erosion with houses collapsing into the surf.

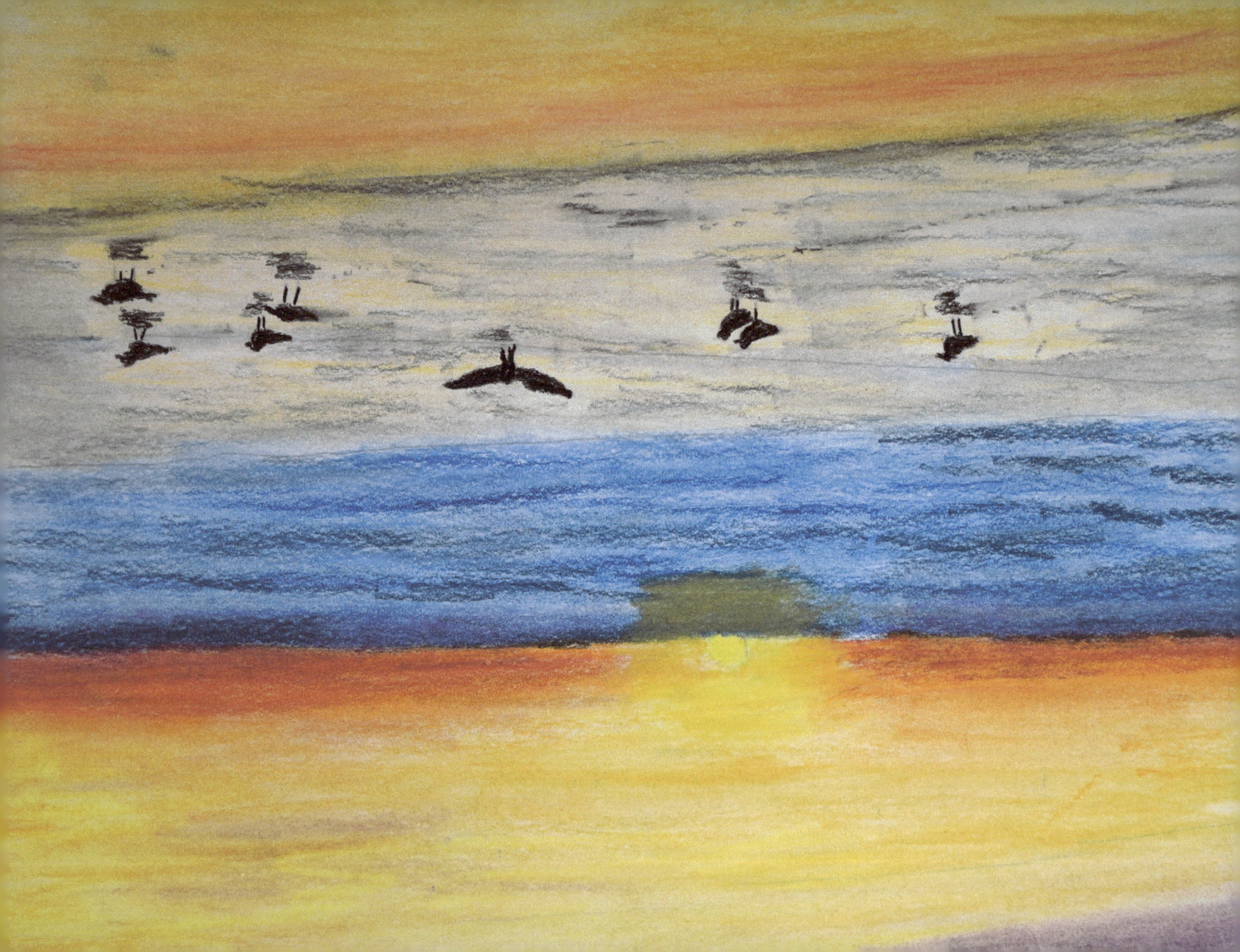

# Anastasia Island Sunrise

Florida was one of the first states to install a coastal setback line.  In 1961 the state legislature passed the Shore and Beach Preservation Act (BSPA), which was strengthened by The Beach and Shore Preservation Act in 1993.  The act establishes coastal construction control lines along sandy beach counties along the coastline of Florida.  The BSPA then prohibits most coastal construction seaward of the control line. The dunes are protected from erosion, by limiting access to narrow walkways, many of which are protected from erosion with boardwalks and bridges.

The result of these laws and their enforcement by the Florida Department of Environmental Protection (DEP), has resulted in a series of setbacks as one proceeds south along St. Augustine Beach.  The area near the Fishing Pier has been heavily eroded with construction closest to the water.  Farther south significant dunes have formed with newer housing progressively farther from the water.  Some have complained about the forming dunes obstructing their views of the ocean, but the dunes stopped the waves from invading these homes during the recent hurricanes, Matthew and Irma, so they are now thankful for their protection.

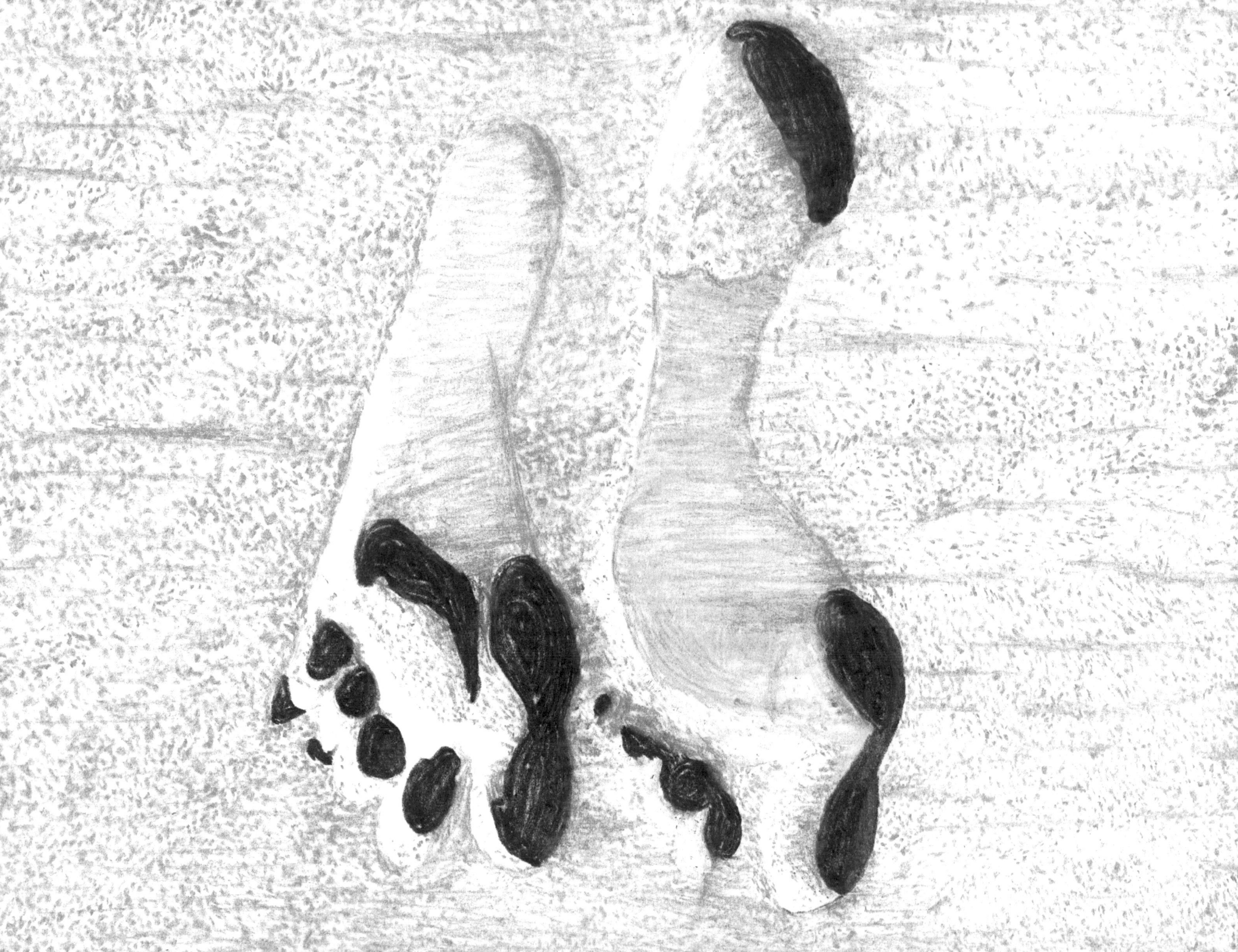

# Lasting Impressions

When Ponce de Leon sighted North America for the first time, near present St Augustine, he thought it was another island and called it La Florida. He came back to settle his new colony, and died trying. A total of 11 settlements were started by Spain and failed before St Augustine was established.

When the Spanish King learned that France had set up Fort Caroline near present Jacksonville, he sent his Admiral, Pedro Menendez to evict the French. He was rebuffed from Fort Caroline by the French fleet, he settled his men on a beach to the south of Fort Caroline, and called the settlement St. Augustine.
The French fleet was conquered by storm, and Menendez captured Fort Caroline and killed most of the French settlers.

Menendez settled St. Augustine with a mix of Spanish, German, Africans, and other European settlers. Some of the settlers married local Indians. St. Augustine was the original "melting pot" before America was formed, having enjoyed the first thanksgiving feast with the local tribe well before the Pilgrims landed at Plymouth Rock, or the British at Jamestown.

Menendez went on to establish 15 more settlements ranging through the present Georgia, the Carolinas and Tennessee. Of these new settlements, all but St. Augustine failed and were abandoned.

The settlement faced Indian uprising, attacks by pirates, the British and American colonies, but survived as the oldest continuously occupied city for Europeans in North America.

We believe that St Augustine survived because of the resiliency of its ethnically diverse population, welcoming new immigrants such as the Minorcans.

The city continues to welcome the new immigrants from such diverse cultures as our Northern Virginia, New York, Pittsburg and Quebec. When we visited looking for a warmer climate to settle, we were met by

When problems strike, this is a city whose settlers help each other. We experienced this when Hurricane Matthew struck, with shelters opening for those who needed them. The community pitched in to help with cleanup of those who were flooded. To help out, one couple put together a Christmas feast for those in need. This has become an annual get-together.

In short, St. Augustine thrives today because it has a frontier spirit, where people are friendly and help out their neighbors, as well as snow birds, those newly arrived and settlers. A Twitter poster summed it up as:

## #staugstrong

www.ingramcontent.com/pod-product-compliance
Lightning Source LLC
Chambersburg PA
CBHW051051180526
45172CB00002B/592